37

GRAPHIC COMMUNICATION

WILEY SERIES ON HUMAN COMMUNICATION

W. A. Mambert
Presenting Technical Ideas: A Guide to Audience Communication

William J. Bowman
Graphic Communication

Herman M. Weisman
Technical Correspondence: A Handbook and Reference Source for the
Technical Professional

John H. Mitchell
Writing for Technical and Professional Journals

JOHN WILEY & SONS, INC., NEW YORK / LONDON / SYDNEY

GRAPHIC
COMMUNICATION

WILLIAM J BOWMAN

NC730.B63   c. 3

Copyright © 1968 by John Wiley & Sons, Inc. All rights reserved. This book or any part thereof must not be reproduced in any form without the written permission of the publisher. Library of Congress Catalog Card Number: 67-29931 Printed in the United States of America GB 471 09 290X

DESIGNED AND ILLUSTRATED By William J. Bowman

To PAULA
   LINNEA
   ARNE
   LUCINDA

913298

EDUCATION

PREFACE

reserve

A picture worth a thousand words must first be a good picture. The difference between words and pictures is the difference between telling and showing, and this book is for the person who is concerned with showing. It is for the technical author seeking visual concepts through which to communicate his ideas, for the illustrator and graphic designer seeking forms to embody those concepts, and for the editor and the publications manager who evaluate and direct the production of the graphic statement. It is also for the specialist in communications technology who is seeking a graphic resource; and most important, for the educator who is seeking to present the language, the design methodology, and the practical substance of graphic communication for others to use.

In practice, graphic communication encompasses a variety of independent disciplines, ranging from technical illustration and cartography to visual education. In all of these diverse fields, graphic thinking is primary, and design is the vehicle which carries the graphic thought to its destination as a graphic statement. This book is therefore concerned with the design of the graphic figure. At the same time, it is necessarily concerned with the language elements available to design, and the communicative purposes toward which design is aimed.

While this material is presented thread by thread, it is to be understood that its meaning lies in the total fabric formed by the interwoven threads; that communicative purpose, visual language, and design logic participate simultaneously in the formation of the graphic figure.

The greater portion of the book is devoted to concrete design examples, in which solutions are offered for a variety of recurrent problems in graphic communication. No effort has been made to separate these examples with respect to field of practice. Rather, they have been organized in terms of their expressive objectives and related in terms of conceptual logic. These design solutions are intended to serve as conceptual models, to be interpreted rather than imitated. With this spirit in mind, they have been executed informally in pencil, rather than in formal media such as ink and airbrush.

In Part I, the graphic figure is presented as a communicative vehicle. Part II reviews visual language as it applies to the design of the graphic figure. Here, form elements and various types of spatial organization are described, and factors of image composition are defined in terms of their expressive functions. As a guide to the design of the graphic figure,

Part III outlines the principles and procedures of visualization. Typical subjects are translated into visual concepts, and then formed into design models. After refinement through visual editing, word and number elements are integrated into the designs. Finally, methods of graphic processing, as the concluding step in the production of the graphic statement, are considered. Parts IV, V, VI, and VII constitute a design library, and provide a resource of graphic concepts applicable to a wide variety of problems encountered in practice. They cover a range of specific communicative aims, and explore a number of problem variations within each aim.

Although color hue can be a potent tool in some complex graphic figures, it will not be included in the scope of this book. Several of the illustrations in part IV, section 1 were executed by Clair Lee and Richard Maruhashi of Stanford Research Institute, for which the author wishes to express his appreciation. Special acknowledgement is due to Rogers Cannell and to Mike Beigler for the assistance and encouragement they supplied during the preparation of this book.

William J. Bowman
Portola Valley, California
January, 1968

CONTENTS

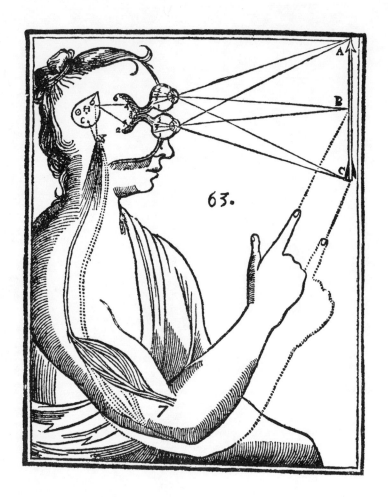

INTRODUCTION

Graphic communication needs no introduction. It has been with us for centuries under a variety of names. Like other visual arts, it employs visual language. Unlike others, it acts as a vehicle for practical communication rather than personal expression. As the knowledge made available by contemporary science and technology grows in quantity and complexity, the need for more effective communicative means becomes correspondingly greater. To meet this need, graphic communication draws upon the natural resources of its own language, and refers to visual experience as a source of principles and values for designing more articulate form. What is introduced, then, is a conceptual logic rather than a technical method; a way of seeing the graphic figure as a visual statement.

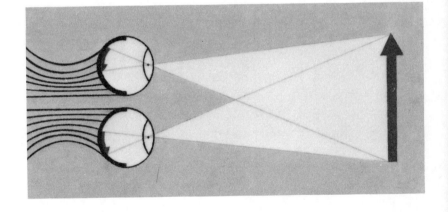

1

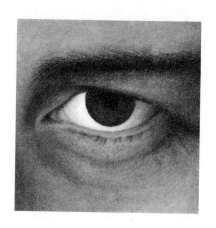

FIGURATIVELY SPEAKING

While the text speaks with words, the graphic figure speaks with form. Although subject matter provides the substance for the figure, what the figure actually says as a visual statement depends more on the communicative aim which shapes this raw material into a purposeful visual idea; and upon the form which embodies and animates that idea. In speaking, however, one says not only what he wants to say but what his language enables him to say. The capabilities and limitations of visual language are themselves decisive factors in determining the kinds of ideas the figure may show about a given subject. This range of communicative potential can be demonstrated by using as an example the human eye, and asking about it the basic questions of *what, how, how much,* and *where.*

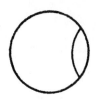

WHAT something is concerns its natural appearance, physical structure, or organization of parts in relation to the whole. While questions in this area often refer to observed realities, they can also concern realities normally unseen as well as abstracted realities. Some relevant questions might be:

APPEARANCE

What are the natural features of the eye as they normally appear? The first figure shows the appearance of the eye by echoing its visual image. Here, qualities of light and shade must be reconciled with local color value to recreate the image. Since the eye alone is the subject, its environment can be omitted.

STRUCTURE

What is the physical structure of the eye beyond what is normally seen? The second figure shows the structure of the eye by representing it as a cross-section view. Its component parts are simplified in their form to clarify the image in terms of its structural essentials.

ORGANIZATION

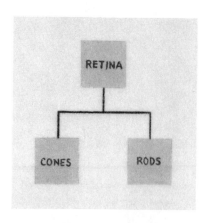

What is the essential organization of the eye's retinal apparatus? The third figure shows organization by reducing the retinal structure to an abstract logic. Natural appearances are irrelevant to the purposes of this image. Linked idea-boxes are used to describe the pattern of interrelated elements.

HOW something acts concerns its physical movement, logic of flow in relation to component parts, or process as a succession of related events. Here, the representation of activity in a static figure requires the use of symbolic motion forms. Questions in this area can concern physical phenomena or idea patterns abstracted from reality:

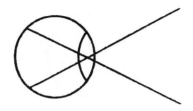

How does light behave as it moves from the external world into the mechanism of the eye? The first figure shows movement within a context of associative symbols. Simple outline shapes serve to identify the lens and retina, while a gray band is used to differentiate and describe the behavior pattern.

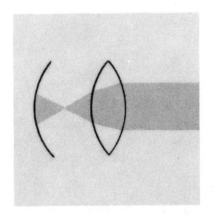

MOVEMENT

How does the eye operate to report physical subjects in the external world? The second figure shows the system by which the image of the subject is produced. Fixed elements are treated as abstract idea-boxes, and are related by a symbolic flow arrow which indicates the passage from cause to effect.

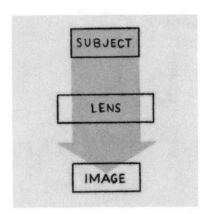

SYSTEM

How does the human body respond to the eye's activity? The third figure shows the process as an abstract idea pattern, in which idea-boxes represent independent events linked in a progressive continuity by symbolic arrow connectors. In this case, arrow symbols indicate procedure rather than motion of the subject.

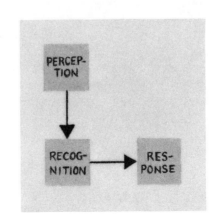

PROCESS

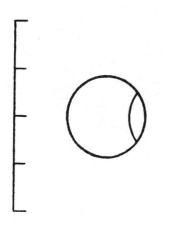

HOW MUCH of something there is concerns its physical size, its numerical quantity, its trend of increase or decrease, or the division of its parts in terms of the whole. The quantitative analysis of a subject involves a process of abstraction, as does its representation in graphic form. Some typical questions in this area might be:

SIZE

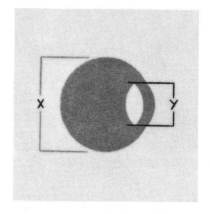

How much vertical space does the eye and its lens occupy? The first figure shows size by independent measurement lines. The eye and lens shapes are extremely simplified, since only their height is relevant to the question and subject association is the only other requirement.

QUANTITY
AND
TREND

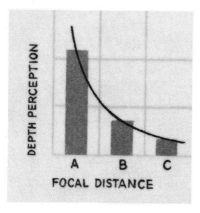

How much depth can the eyes perceive at varying distances? The second figure shows quantity and trend as coordinate values, in which degree of perception is measured at fixed points on a distance scale. The context is abstract. Perception quantities are represented by abstract bar extensions, and a linear curve generalizes the trend of decreasing perception.

DIVISION

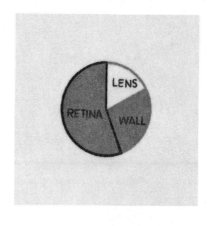

How much of the eye's internal surface is occupied by each major part? The third figure shows division in terms of an abstract, circular whole. While the white lens area is an independent segment, the outlined retinal area represents a segment which occupies a part of the larger gray wall segment.

WHERE something is concerns its natural area, its environmental location, or its position with respect to other individual elements. While the distinction between these three aspects is often subtle, the basic questions which relate to them can differ considerably in their functional objectives. For example:

Where is the natural area of the eye in relation to its physical surroundings? The first figure shows the eye's area by representing it in direct association with neighboring physical features. Area, in this sense, refers to the space in which the subject is physically situated.

AREA

Where is the exact location of the eye in terms of its overall environment? The second figure shows location by reducing the subject's form to a symbol and representing its distance from recognizable environmental characteristics. Here, spatial relationship rather than physical situation is the defining context.

LOCATION

Where is the position of the eye with respect to other sensory receptors? The third figure shows position by representing the subject symbol in spatial relation to a network of companion elements rather than to an overall environment. The graphic context is entirely symbolic.

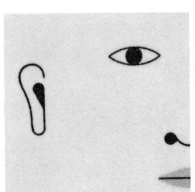

POSITION

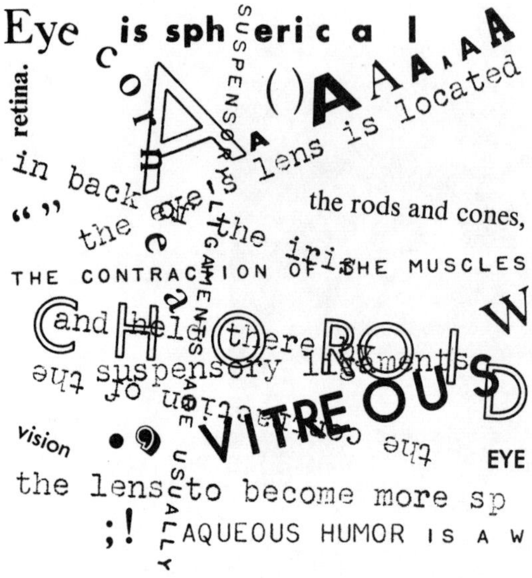

II

Eye is spherical

retina.

SUSPENSORY

( ) A A A A A

lens is located

in back

the rods and cones,

"" the the iris

THE CONTRACTION OF THE MUSCLES

and there

C H O RO W

suspensory ligaments

VITREOUS D

vision

the lens to become more sp

;! AQUEOUS HUMOR IS A W

EYE

VISUAL LANGUAGE

Fluency in visual expression, as in verbal expression, derives not only from practical experience but also from a knowledge and understanding of the language itself and of the principles guiding its effective use. As in other languages, visual language has resources and capabilities peculiar to its own nature—a vocabulary of form elements, a grammar of spatial organization, an idiom of volumetric perspective, and a syntax for phrasing the image. While in the fine arts visual language often becomes an end in itself, to be explored for all it is worth, in applied arts such as engineering drafting and commercial art its use is constrained by conventions of the factory and the marketplace. While graphic communication does not suffer these constraints, its own functions impose other demands which will be considered in this review of visual language.

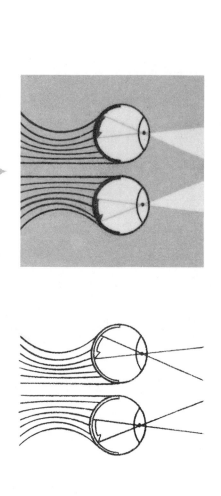

FORM VOCABULARY

To design the graphic figure it is first necessary to know what one has to design with—the constructive elements, their capabilities, and their limitations. Casual analysis shows that form derives from five basic elements: point, line, shape, color (here, color value), and texture. These elements constitute the form vocabulary available to graphic communication. While the draftsman relies mainly on line to construct his figure, the graphic illustrator is not bound by the conventions or the industrial objectives of the draftsman, and need not limit his form to line alone. Although one could arbitrarily restrict his speech to the argot of the short-order kitchen, there is no more reason for him to do so than for the graphic illustrator to limit his vocabulary to an argot of line. Such arbitrary limitation can only sterilize the form of the graphic figure. Its design, therefore, should take place with a full recognition of the form resources which may be utilized to achieve the expressive purpose. In constructing form, design tends to employ informal media such as pencil, leaving formal media to the execution phase. In both design and execution, however, an effective graphic statement requires an effective form vocabulary of *point, line, shape, color value,* and *texture.*

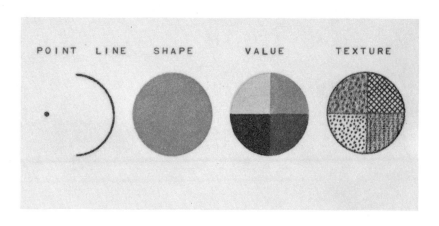

POINT   LINE   SHAPE   VALUE   TEXTURE

POINT is in the theoretical sense non-dimensional, and shows location, position, or focus. As a figurative element it is characterized by a convergence of form or visual impact into a center that attracts and fixes the eye's focus.

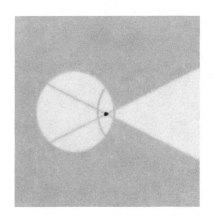

In practice, a point can vary with respect to size, structure, and color value. It can also act as a symbol, representing a specific subject or idea. A point can be elaborated or enlarged around its center for identification or impact. As a visual center, it can be suggested by a circular form or by an intersection of lines without being physically present. Letters and numbers, as participating form within the figure often act visually as points.

As a structural element, a point can act as a center for circular form, as a terminal for converging form, or as a vanishing point within a perspective framework which determines the direction of receding planes.

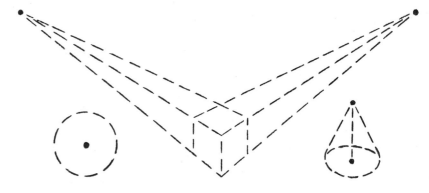

11

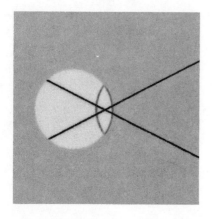

LINE is one-dimensional in character and shows direction, extension, or movement. As a form element, linear structure can also be employed to describe a path or a route; or to indicate a boundary or a division.

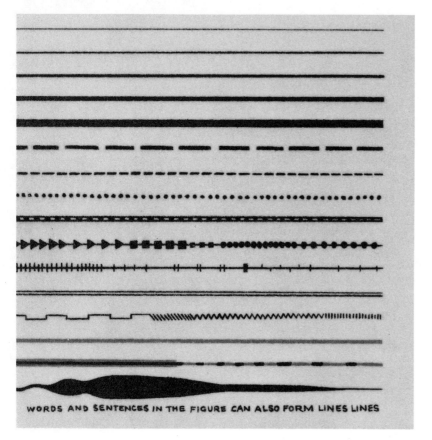

WORDS AND SENTENCES IN THE FIGURE CAN ALSO FORM LINES LINES

Linear form can vary in weight, length, structure, character, value, and course. A major quality of line is its directional capability. In this role, it can also indicate motion. Lines can have lapses or interruptions. Continuities of line fragments or points are "completed" by the eye as linear form. A line can be symbolic in meaning. Varying in width, it can also indicate changes in magnitude. As visual elements, words and sentences can form lines.

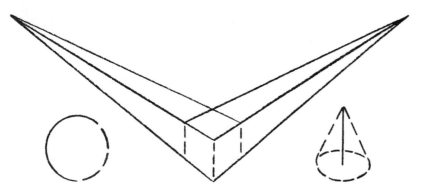

As a structural element, a line can be used to establish a constructive axis for other form, to outline plane form, or to describe a perspective framework for volumetric form.

SHAPE is two-dimensional form. Occupying lateral, or flat space within the picture plane, it acts as plane form to show contour, area, outline, enclosure, or edge.

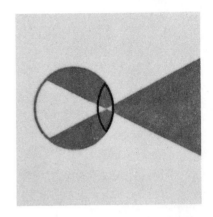

Shape quality derives from the structuring of its edge, and varies with respect to size, distribution of weight, position, and regularity (or irregularity) of edge. A shape can be constructed solid or in outline form. Enclosing space with surrounding form can create a negative shape. Groupings of words and numbers can act as shapes. By utilizing associative characteristics, shapes can also act as symbols. Certain combinations of form can, as a group, suggest a simple shape and act as such insofar as the eye is concerned.

As structural elements, shapes can be used in conjunction with one another to create volumes, particularly within a linear perspective framework.

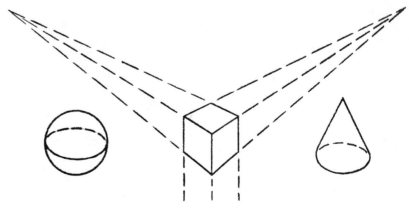

13

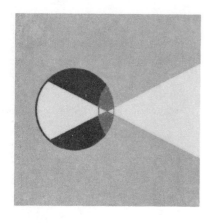

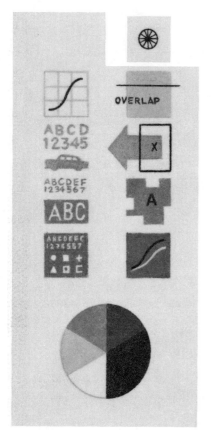

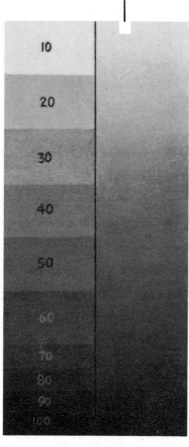

VALUE is a quality of color which refers to its degree of darkness or lightness. In the absence of hues (red, yellow, blue, etc.), color values become simply shades of gray. In graphics, the impression of gray is created by a concentration of minute dots which at the eye's distance seem to blend with the intervening white spaces. The resultant shade depends on the relative size and density of the dots.

Very light values are useful for providing a subtle containing ground for groups of related elements or for a detailed figure. Light values define more clearly an area or structure, while permitting detailed black form to be superimposed. Light-middle values are dark enough to describe detailed form yet light enough to permit superimposed black form. Middle values can be used to construct fine form or to show large reversed (white) form. Dark-middle values provide a contrasting ground for small reversed form or for subordinated black form. Dark and very dark values are useful in combination with other values, where range is required for differentiation.

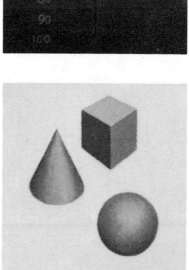

As a structural element, color value is a useful means for describing volumetric form, through light and shadow. This can be done with solid planes of differing value, or with graduated tones.

14

TEXTURE is a quality of surface structure or pattern. Although deriving from the suggestion of physical surface constitution, tactility as a visual quality is "felt" by the eye rather than the hand; and is created by the massing of small particles into an arrangement whose visual character derives from their combination as a whole.

Textural character varies in terms of the structure of its individual elements and the spaces between them. The manner of arrangement of the elements is also a factor. Generally, these elements can be composed in either a regular or an irregular pattern. Textures can be abstract, symbolic, or descriptive. Like other form, texture can vary in its color value.

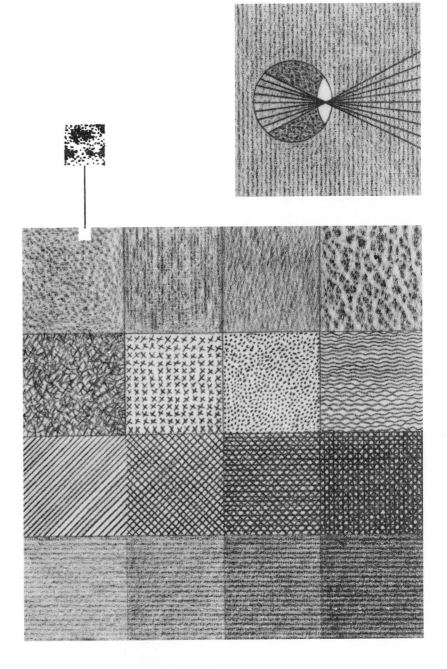

As a structural element, texture can be used to show the quality of physical surfaces. As such, it can be used in conjunction with other form elements, particularly color value.

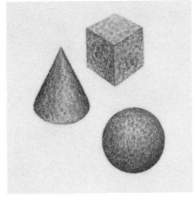

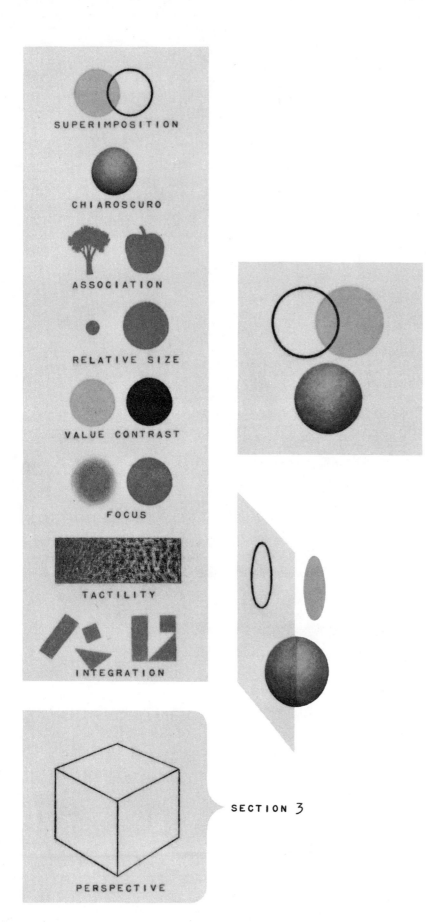

SUPERIMPOSITION

CHIAROSCURO

ASSOCIATION

RELATIVE SIZE

VALUE CONTRAST

FOCUS

TACTILITY

INTEGRATION

PERSPECTIVE

SECTION 3

2
SPACE GRAMMAR

Whatever the form of the figure, to exist at all it must exist upon a surface, or picture plane. Physically, the picture plane is simply the page area on which one works; but in the design sense, it functions as a two-dimensional space. Seeing the page as an imaginary plane, like a pane of glass, provides a space orientation for the elements of the figure which can then be conceived to be located not only upon the picture plane, but behind it; multiplying its content capability by adding a dimension of depth. While depth is not always desirable, it is always potential. The picture, as an artificial image, necessarily echoes visual imagery and needs only a familiar spacial cue to go inward. Depth can thus be created through form characteristics which act as spatial cues. It can also be avoided by the absence of spatial cues. This means that spatial quality in the graphic figure is defined by the form that it organizes. Thus, form elements should be designed not only in terms of their individual meanings, but in terms of the spatial order necessary to relate those meanings to one another within a single, coherent image. In practice, spatial organization can be *plane, multi-plane,* or *continuous,* depending on the needs of the problem. Linear perspective will be examined in the next section.

PLANE space is that in which the form is contained entirely on the picture plane, and is thus flat both in structure and in arrangement. As a two-dimensional design framework, plane space is best achieved through form organization in which spatial cues are absent. Forms therefore appear to be objects *on* the page rather than images *in* it. There are various ways of keeping form on a flat plane, to avoid ambiguities in meaning which might arise in certain figures if they were spatially disunited. They include:

1. The use of form whose essential character is plane rather than irregular or oblique.

2. Related forms joined on a common edge rather than overlapped.

3. Dissimilar forms connected rather than overlapped or spatially separated.

4. Parallel association of recognizable subjects or symbols, as they would appear in reality.

5. Similar size or scale for forms of dissimilar physical structure.

6. Uniformity of edge character, to achieve focal similarity rather than the spatial quality of unequal focus.

7. Even or uniform textural structure, to avoid the suggestion of a receding physical surface.

8. Integration of dissimilar or irregular form elements to compose a recognizably plane form.

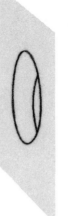
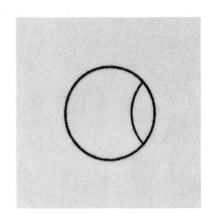

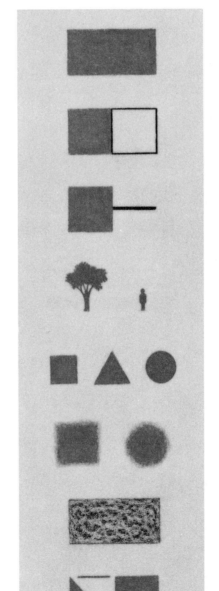

PLANE ECHO

CONTINUITY

CONNECTION

PARALLEL ASSOCIATION

EQUAL SIZE

FOCAL SIMILARITY

EVEN TEXTURE

INTEGRATION

17

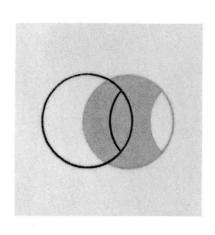

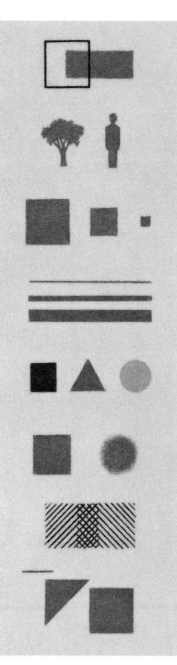

SUPERIMPOSITION

DISTANCE ASSOCIATION

UNEQUAL SIZE

UNEQUAL WEIGHT

VALUE CONTRAST

FOCAL DISSIMILARITY

TEXTURAL OVERLAP

DISINTEGRATION

MULTI-PLANE space disengages the form of the figure into two (or more) separate planes. One is the picture plane, and the other is a secondary plane located behind the picture plane but parallel to it. Thus one plane appears to be closer to the eye, or *in front* of the other. While the form of many figures is necessarily plane in character, visual coherence often requires their organization into separate planes through the use of spatial cues such as:

1. Overlapping or superimposed forms, to spatially separate the planes on which they appear.

2. Distance association of recognizable forms, through differences between their apparent size and their known size.

3. Unequal size or scale of forms with similar structure, to suggest distance association.

4. Unequal weight of linear forms, again to suggest the distance association of apparently similar forms.

5. Contrasting color values, in which the weaker value seems to recede spatially.

6. Dissimilar focus, to suggest atmospheric recession of the blurred form.

7. Overlapping and contradicting textures, rather than reinforcing textural patterns.

8. Form elements which are disintegrated in terms of compositional relationships.

CONTINUOUS space is volumetric in nature, in which form is seen to extend inward from the picture plane in an unbroken fashion to create an illusion of spatial mass. Volumetric form, then, is seen *through* the window pane rather than *on* it. Its spatial cues include:

1. Chiaroscuro, or the modeling effect of light and darkness.

2. Association of forms with reality, and adjusting known size relationships to suggest distance between them.

3. Separation of forms in depth by value contrast, the lighter form receding the farthest into the light background.

4. Focal dissimilarity, through the diffusion of edges of the receding form.

5. Superimposition of closer forms over farther ones.

6. Reduction in scale of textural surfaces as they recede in depth.

Convincing spatial volume depends upon the mutual interaction of many spatial cues in conjunction with one another, whenever the occasion permits. The strongest implication of continuous form and space is achieved when all available cues are used together within a *linear perspective* framework. This method for constructing volumetric form will be explained in the following section.

CHIAROSCURO

DISTANCE ASSOCIATION

VALUE CONTRAST

FOCAL DISSIMILARITY

SUPERIMPOSITION

TEXTURAL RECESSION

THE PERSPECTIVE IDIOM

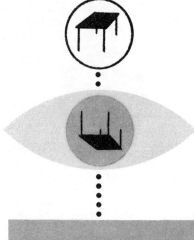

3

THE PERSPECTIVE IDIOM

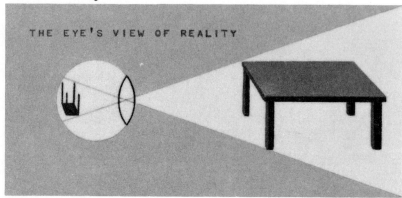

THE EYE'S VIEW OF REALITY

If plane form derives from the character of the page, volumetric form derives from the nature of the eye's image. Volumetric form is more complex than plane form since it must reconcile three-dimensional features with a two-dimensional surface. In doing so, it borrows upon the eye's view of reality. The human eye interprets natural reality into a flat, retinal image (inverted by the eye, but mentally corrected to conform to reality) in which the apparent sizes of objects vary in direct proportion to their proximity to the eye. Volumetric perspective is built upon this principle. Briefly, its elements include:

1. The picture plane.
2. The horizon line, or eye level with respect to the picture plane.
3. The focal point, or location of visual focus on the horizon line.
4. The viewpoint, or position from which the object is seen.
5. The vanishing points, which establish the direction of receding form and show its position, or perspective.

In constructing the perspective figure, its orientation to the picture plane can be *parallel, angular,* or *oblique.*

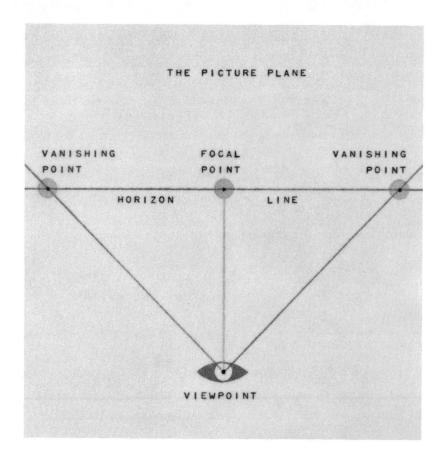

THE PICTURE PLANE

VANISHING POINT   FOCAL POINT   VANISHING POINT

HORIZON   LINE

VIEWPOINT

PARALLEL perspective is that in which two of the three spatial dimensions (a frontal plane) of the volumetric figure are in parallel relation to the picture plane. The third dimension recedes toward the focal point which in this case performs the function of the vanishing point (VP). In general, parallel perspective best shows the face, or frontal-plane aspect of form opposite the eye-level, emphasizing the object's parallel relationship to the picture plane.

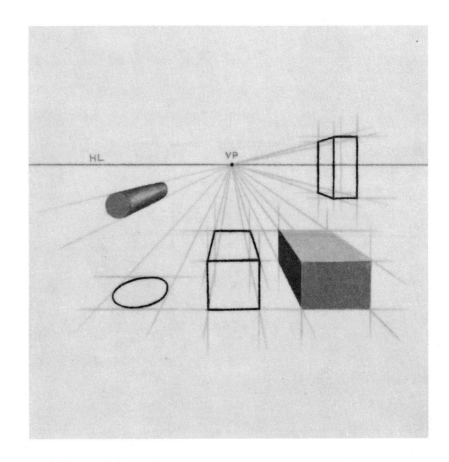

Parallel perspective is also useful in representing internal volume, since this position usually permits a maximum view of interior surfaces. It is necessary to note, however, that certain forms of subject matter, such as plans, require the use of mechanical techniques to be accurately translated into perspective figures. In the accompanying example, plan and elevation views of the subject are projected into a three-dimensional structure by relating its planes to the viewpoint (V) and vanishing point (VP) as indicated. The horizon line (HL) bisects the figure, permitting a full interior view.

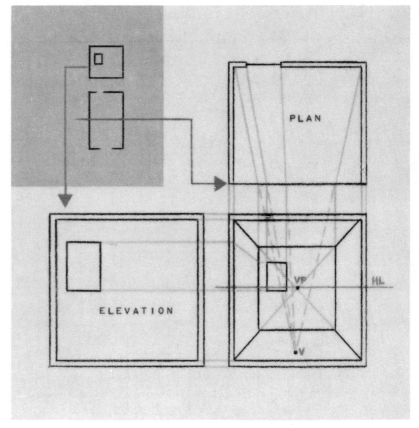

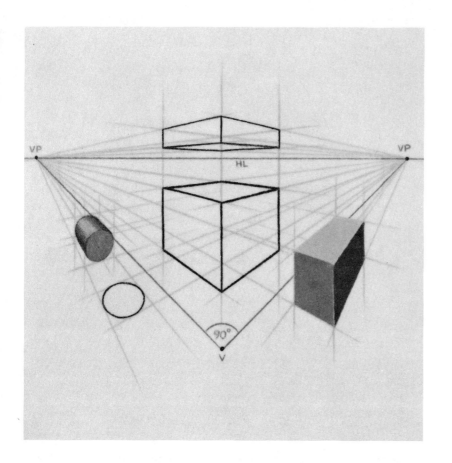

ANGULAR perspective is that in which two of the three spatial dimensions of the volumetric figure are in angular relation to the picture plane, and only the third (the vertical dimension) remains parallel to it. The two angular planes recede toward two vanishing points (VP) previously established by constructing a right angle upon the viewpoint (V) and extending the two sides of the angle until they intersect the horizon line (HL). In general, angular perspective emphasizes the spatial character, or sculptural aspect of the object.

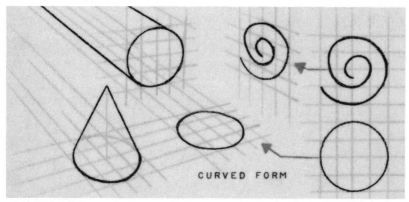

CURVED FORM

Curved form presents a special problem. It can be solved, however, by relating the curve to a rectangular grid which itself is set into perspective as a visual guide for constructing the curve. In perspective, circles become near-ellipses.

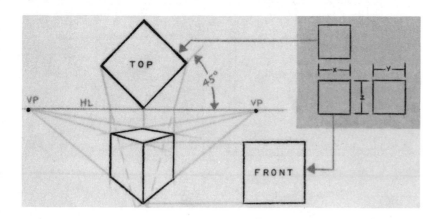

The translation of working drawings into angular perspective follows the same procedure as in parallel perspective, with the exception that the top view is set at an angular position relative to the horizon line (HL). This position is determined by the degree of angularity to the picture plane desired in the final figure.

OBLIQUE perspective is that in which all three spatial dimensions of the volume are in angular relation to the picture plane. The entire figure is located well above or below the horizon line. Two planes recede toward the horizon line vanishing points (VP) as in angular perspective. The third recedes toward the focal point (FP) which is moved to a position below the horizon line (if the figure is below it) or to a position above the horizon line (if the figure is above it). The focal point is located at a distance from the horizon line which is proportional to the figure's degree of angularity to the picture plane.

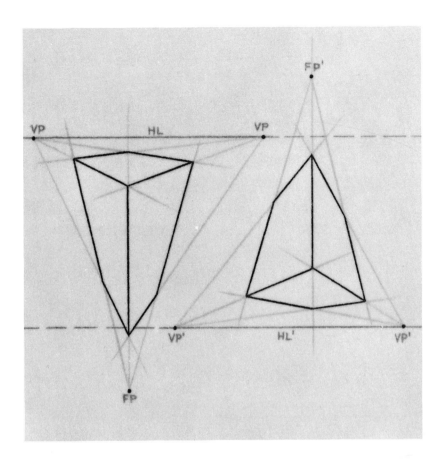

Oblique perspective, while showing the sculptural aspect of the object, emphasizes its recession into deep space away from the eye-level. Oblique perspective is the most difficult of the three perspective methods, and fortunately, the least employed. Nevertheless, when used in an appropriate situation, and in conjunction with chiaroscuro, the illusion of spatial mass created can have considerable visual impact.

23

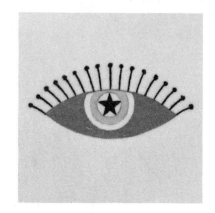

4

PHRASING THE IMAGE

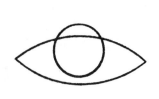

(INSUFFICIENT FORM)

(EXCESSIVE FORM)

(INEFFECTIVE FORM)

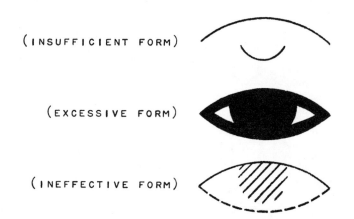

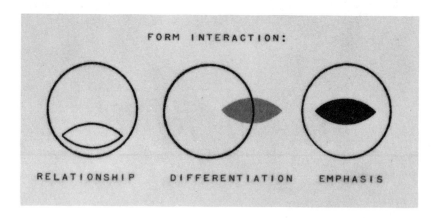

FORM INTERACTION:

RELATIONSHIP   DIFFERENTIATION   EMPHASIS

Form is not a decorative facade, but the architecture of the figure as a meaningful image. Elegant form vocabulary and dramatic spatial organization are useless if the graphic figure fails to present the intended statement. Like the verbal phrase, the visual phrase created by a figure means no more than the ideas it conveys. To be articulate, its form must function. How well it functions depends on its selection and treatment. Not enough form, too much form, or the wrong kind of form can impair communication. Moreover, how a form acts is as important as what it is. Forms interact in the figure as words do in the sentence. Each is affected by its context. Similarities in form character and position can associate elements into a visual relationship, and convey the idea of related meaning. Conversely, form dissimilarities and dissociations can produce visual differentiation, both in the image and in its pattern of meanings. Also, a form element with a strong visual character in company with other weaker elements can achieve visual emphasis, adding importance to its meaning. In phrasing the image, *relationship*, *differentiation*, and *emphasis* serve as the primary modes of visual interaction. These are the basic ways in which the image elements function to create an articulate visual statement.

RELATIONSHIP concerns the ways in which form elements are brought into visual association with one another, so that they are connected in meaning. Since a visually related figure is easier to assimilate as a unified idea, a relating framework is generally to be sought. This framework may be either suggested or constructed. Within the figure itself interdependent or like elements can be related by more specific visual means:

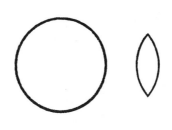

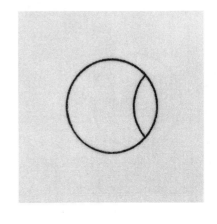

1. Physical similarity in basic form structure which overrides differences in detail.

2. Similarity in tonal value which relates both similar and dissimilar form structures.

3. Organizational continuity, through the alignment of elements.

4. Similarity in quantitative mass, or size, of the related elements.

5. Spatial continuity, in terms of arrangement within a single plane.

6. Association by the use of similar textures.

7. Relating of different elements by enclosing them with an external form.

8. Relationship as a product of the functional interconnection of elements by secondary forms.

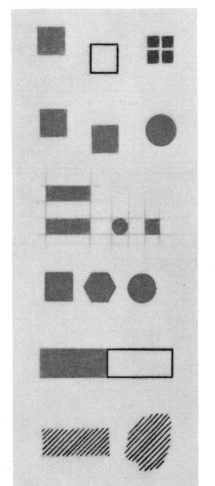

PHYSICAL

TONAL

ORGANIZATIONAL

QUANTITATIVE

SPATIAL

TEXTURAL

EXTERNAL

FUNCTIONAL

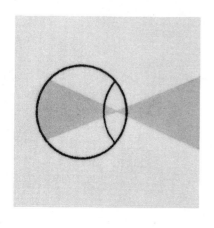

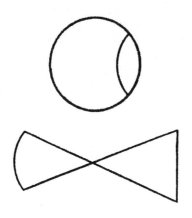

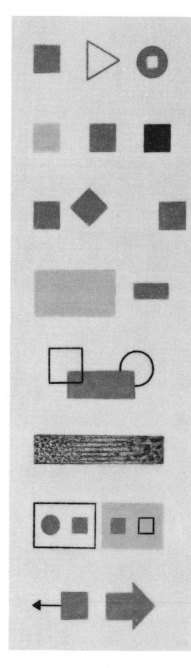

PHYSICAL

TONAL

ORGANIZATIONAL

QUANTITATIVE

SPATIAL

TEXTURAL

EXTERNAL

FUNCTIONAL

DIFFERENTIATION concerns the ways in which form elements can be visually dissociated with regard to dissimilarities in identity and function. While diversity of form is necessary to an articulate figure, elements may be differentiated in one respect and related in another. Specifically, differentiation may be achieved in a variety of ways:

1. Physical differences in basic form structure, both external and internal.

2. Differences in tonal value, within a group of structurally related elements. A scale of emphasis is also present.

3. Dissociated organization, with respect to position and distance of elements.

4. Different quantitative measurement, or size.

5. Spatial separation, through superimposition of form elements in multi-plane space.

6. Differences in the quality of textural patterns.

7. Dissociation of element groups by enclosing them with separated external forms.

8. Differentiation as a product of the symbolic function of the forms; in this case, opposite movements.

EMPHASIS concerns the dominance and subordination of form elements in the figure, and reflects their relative importance rather than merely their differences; which could otherwise be equal in impact. While emphasis is not always essential to the structure of the figure, it can often serve to focus and heighten its meaning. There are different ways to create visual emphasis:

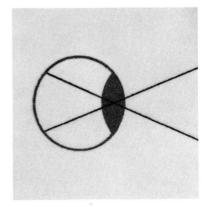

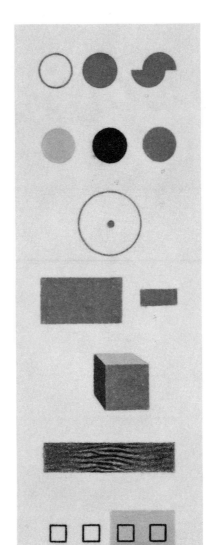

1. Physical dominance, through combined mass and unity (center form).

PHYSICAL

2. Dominance of tonal value (center form).

TONAL

3. Focal dominance of center in relation to circular form.

ORGANIZATIONAL

4. Impact of larger quantity.

QUANTITATIVE

5. Spatial proximity of frontal plane of perspective figure.

SPATIAL

6. Sharpened textural quality (center area).

TEXTURAL

7. External enclosure of important elements in a sequence.

EXTERNAL

8. Functional emphasis as a result of the symbolic action of forms; here, a motion form emphasizing its terminal element.

FUNCTIONAL

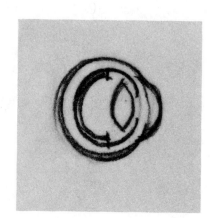

III

THE GRAPHIC STATEMENT

Visual language is not an end in itself. Form, space, and visual interaction are simply means through which to visualize ideas. Visualization begins with a definition of purpose. Relevant subject matter is applied to this purpose and translated into a visual concept; usually in sketch form. A design is then constructed, in which a full range of visual language is used to develop and refine the visual concept into a figure model. After visual editing and the integration of word and number meanings into the design model, the figure is executed in formal media and reproduced as a graphic statement. Concept, design, and production—these are the three basic steps in the visualization process. In this process, design is the central function, and the critical factor in determining the ultimate value of the figure as a graphic statement.

1

VISUAL TRANSLATION

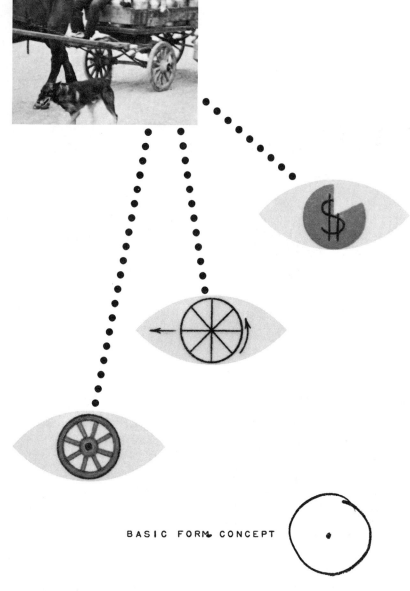

BASIC FORM CONCEPT

CONCEPT LEVELS:

OBJECTIVE   SYMBOLIC   ABSTRACT

In everyday life the meaning of a thing can vary in relation to the way in which it is seen and understood. The farmer, for example, sees the wheel of his wagon as a physical object. The engineer who designed it sees it as a mechanical problem. The merchant who sold it sees it as a financial profit. Thus, while the farmer's view is objective, the engineer symbolizes his view as a plan; and the merchant abstracts his view into dollars and cents. Similarly, the subject of the graphic figure can be seen and represented in different ways, depending on its communicative aim. But how does this visual translation take place? Before a wheel is constructed a working drawing is necessary. Before a graphic figure is constructed, a "thinking" drawing is necessary to determine its basic framework as a visual idea. This thinking drawing, or sketch, is rudimentary and conceptual in nature. Ignoring precision and refinement, it seeks to translate the essentials of the problem into a visual skeleton. It builds upon a general form concept, to which specific elements are added to identify the idea and its level of meaning. Such meaning is defined not only by what is shown and how, but also by what is not shown. As in the view of the wheel, the view of the figure can be *objective*, *symbolic*, or *abstract*.

OBJECTIVE translation shows the idea in terms of visual reality. While the photograph is perhaps the purest example of objectivity, the figure can often enhance the physical character of the subject through exaggeration or simplification. Visual modification, moreover, is frequently necessary to the communicative purpose.

The first figure translates the plan views of an object into a volumetric mass, to show its anticipated appearance.

The second figure translates the observed features of a physical object into a total volumetric outline, to show both its seen and its unseen structure simultaneously.

The third figure translates the box dimensions of the first problem into a volumetric form, and adds a relating bracket to show its size in height.

The fourth figure translates a contour map into a physical surface description, to show the areas in the U.S. where mountains occur.

PROBLEM:

TO SHOW APPEARANCE

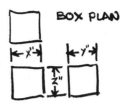

BOX PLAN

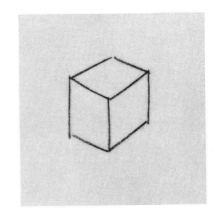

PROBLEM:

TO SHOW STRUCTURE

(PHYSICAL OBJECT)

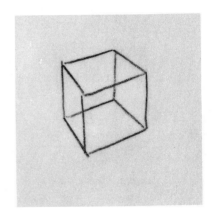

PROBLEM:

TO SHOW SIZE

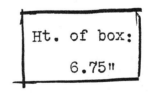

Ht. of box: 6.75"

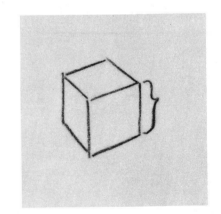

PROBLEM:

TO SHOW AREA

(CONTOUR MAP)

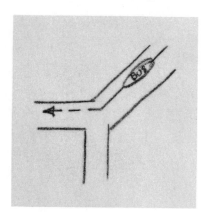

(ROAD MAP)

SYMBOLIC translation removes the idea from a context of natural reality, retaining only the visual features which are essential to its identity and eliminating those which are unnecessary to its meaning in the figure. The symbol itself can be associative or conventional; that is, a visual abbreviation of something seen or known, or a non-representational form whose meaning is defined by convention.

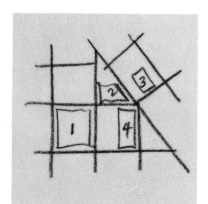

PROBLEM:

TO SHOW POSITION

```
1. 233 Central St.
2. 1704 4th St.
3. 1836 4th St.
4. 1797 5th St.
```

The first figure translates a city road map into a local street diagram, to show the movement pattern of the subject (a vehicle) within it.

The second figure translates a list of addresses into a symbolic context of blocks and streets, to show their positions relative to one another.

PROBLEM:

TO SHOW LOCATION

```
...cities of the
United States with
a total population
over 100,000...
```

The third figure translates text information into points within an abbreviated geographic outline, to show the location of information items.

The fourth figure translates a set of subject functions into a schematic diagram, to show the system which they produce. Here, the flow arrow is the dominant element, and establishes a symbolic context.

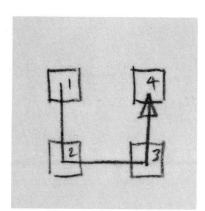

PROBLEM:

TO SHOW SYSTEM

```
CROP CYCLE

1. Plant
2. Fertilize
3. Harvest
4. Market
```

ABSTRACT translation presents the idea in terms of pure visual logic, independent of any associations with specific objects in the real world. It also lends itself to problems in which the technical content or its interpretation is itself abstract (as in mathematical material). Abstract form can also act as an organizing device, without specific meaning.

The first figure translates a sequence of subject phases into a chain of idea-boxes, to show the process they constitute. Here, arrow symbols are subordinate to the overall abstract context.

The second figure translates the elements and parts of a subject outline into a network of interconnected idea-boxes, to show their logic of organization.

The third figure translates numerical data into a coordinate scale, representing both the extension and the interrelation of data values to show their quantity and trend in time.

The fourth figure translates a table of numerical percentages into a segmented shape, to show the proportional division of the total amount.

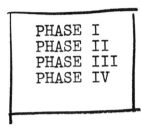

PHASE I
PHASE II
PHASE III
PHASE IV

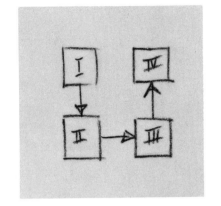

PROBLEM:

TO SHOW ORGANIZATION

SUBJECT X
  A. First element
    1. First part
    2. Second part
  B. Second element
    1. First part
    2. Second part

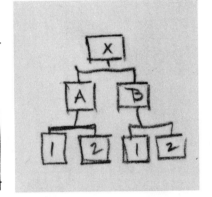

PROBLEM:

TO SHOW QUANTITY
AND TREND

Item	'35	'45	'55	'65
A	12	18	23	32
B	16	24	29	38
C	21	28	35	42
D	26	..	..	..

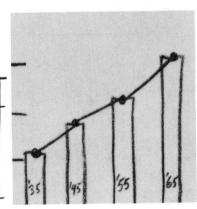

PROBLEM:

TO SHOW DIVISION

Part	%
A	13
B	25
C	62
Total	100

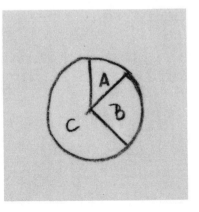

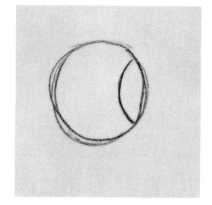

2

DESIGNING THE STATEMENT

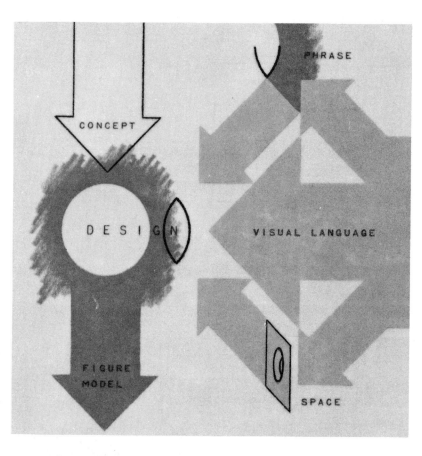

The visual concept provides a skeleton for the graphic figure. The next step is the design of the figure model which will provide this conceptual skeleton with a functioning body. In the preceding pages, subject matter elements have already been identified and translated into the figurative concept within a designated level of visual meaning. Each element must now be given a form character which clearly shows what it is and how it operates in the figure. A full range of visual language should be considered. A form vocabulary must be selected, and tested to assure the effectiveness of its interaction. This can be done by using the vocabulary to represent a typical phrase drawn from the context of the figure. In addition, the spatial organization of the figure must be resolved so that the correct spatial cues can be built into the form structure. Form and space are then integrated into a comprehensive design, which serves as a figure model, or working guide for the production of the graphic statement. Throughout the design process, communicative aim provides a constant frame of reference against which to weigh decisions of form selection. In this section the design process will be applied to figure examples covering thirteen basic communicative aims: *appearance, structure, organization, movement, system, process, size, quantity, trend, division, area, location,* and *position.*

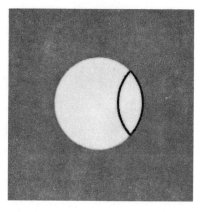

APPEARANCE concerns the natural features of a subject as they are seen by the eye under normal circumstances. In this example, the concept suggests the appearance of a box as a physical mass. Its elements include the enclosing planes of the volume, only three of which are visible under conditions of reality. The level of meaning, or context of this figure is objective.

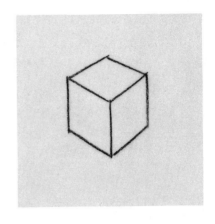

This design aims at pictorial representation. The form vocabulary is graduated shading, based on an imaginary light source and reflections which enable the planes of the box to be differentiated. For this reason, corner edges are emphasized at certain key places. At other places, edges between adjacent planes are blended to preserve their relationship to the whole volume. This shading, edge description, and blending utilize the chiaroscuro technique, which acts here to reinforce the essential perspective structure. Perspective is angular, and the figure is centered to emphasize its forward thrust in space and its recession in depth; to maximize the impact of its physical features.

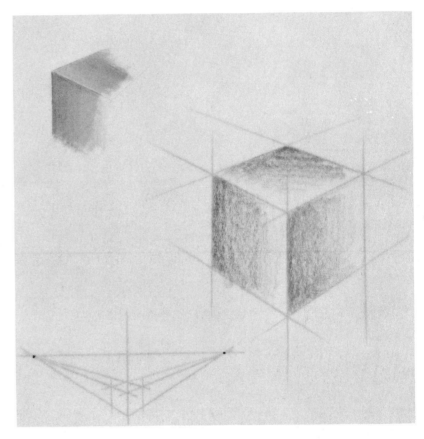

In execution, this figure model will be interpreted through the medium of airbrush, which will serve to refine the quality of its graduated shading. Element identifications are not necessary, therefore no allowance has been made in its design for word forms.

35

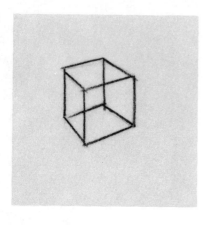

STRUCTURE concerns the essential physical constitution of a subject, beyond that which can normally be seen. In this sketch, the concept indicates the external structure of the cube object by describing all of its corners and edges, including those which would normally be hidden behind its body. Thus, its figurative elements are the twelve edges which describe its volumetric form. The context is objective, despite modification of its appearance.

Here, design aims at linear representation. Form vocabulary consists of line types: solid for visible edges, and shaded for those which are invisible. If all were black, the figure would become ambiguous. Thus, there are two related frameworks in the design—one black, and the other differentiated (and subordinated) as gray. Both are part of a total spatial organization set in angular perspective. The forward vertical edge is offset to the left so as not to coincide and interfere with its opposite edge in the rear.

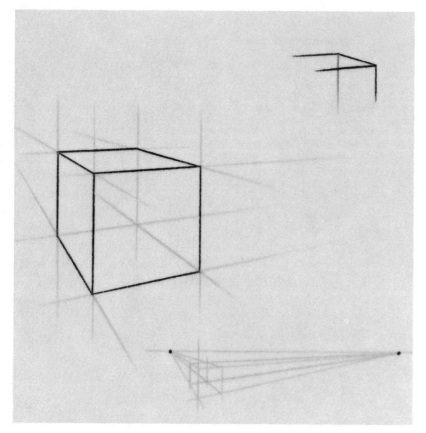

The execution of this figure will be in ink, which will sharpen the line quality beyond that of the figure model. At that time, the gray lines could be interpreted through fine dotted lines, to simplify reproduction processing. Element identifications will not be necessary, and no provisions for word forms have been made in the design.

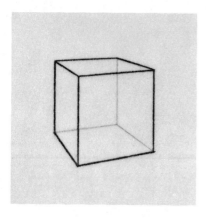

ORGANIZATION concerns the logical interrelation of elements of a subject in terms of the whole. In this case, the concept reflects the three levels of organization present in the subject outline: The subject, its primary elements, and the secondary parts of each element. The context is abstract.

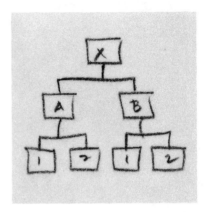

This design aims at a formal composition. Its vocabulary includes rectangular shapes (shaded, to contain word meanings) and black line connectors which serve to build a pattern of relationship between the shapes. The shapes act as abstract idea-boxes, and are effectively differentiated from the lines by their solidity and their shaded gray value. The whole structure itself is arranged on a flat plane, to maintain a context of parallel meaning among its elements. Idea-boxes are similar in size to avoid spatial cues which might create ambiguities in image meaning. For the same reason, form structure is horizontal and vertical, and parallel alignment is used wherever possible.

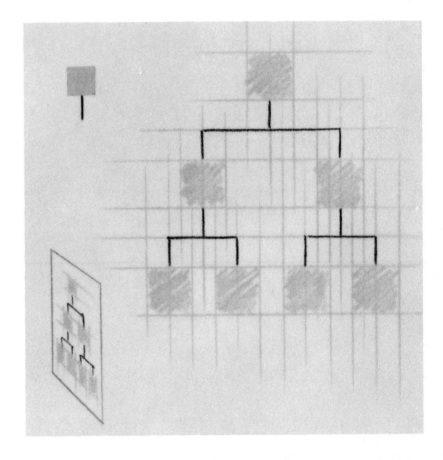

At a later time, word and number forms will be placed within the gray boxes to identify them and complete their meaning. Thus, the design of the figure model anticipates the space required for such additional forms. Ink and acetate will be used to construct the lines and shapes, respectively.

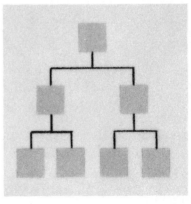

37

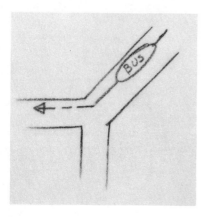

MOVEMENT concerns the physical action or behavior pattern of a subject in motion. Here, the concept visualizes the route and movement of a vehicle within a local street intersection. Thus, subject elements include the vehicle, its pattern of motion, and the street system. Since the idea concerns movement rather than physical features, the forms are symbolic rather than objective.

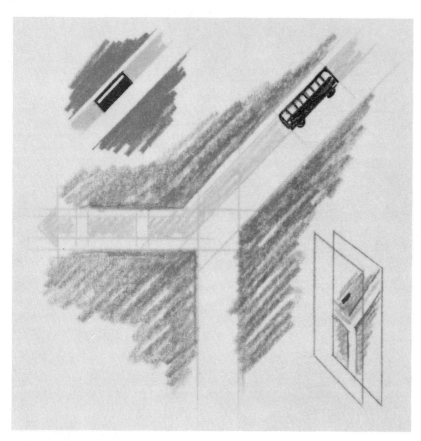

Design in this figure seeks to build a symbolic diagram. The vocabulary consists primarily of shapes (linear, in the case of the route form), related to one another in their alignment and differentiated in structure and color value with respect to their specific meanings. The black vehicle form is emphasized, and becomes the forward element in a multi-plane spatial organization so that it will appear to be on top of the gray route form. The gray route form itself is light, to convey the intangible quality of the motion it indicates. The street pattern is represented as negative (white) form to permit maximum value contrast between the compounded elements of the figure.

To complete the meaning of this figure, word labels will be added to identify the less obvious or generalized parts of the figure model. Execution will employ ink and acetate, to assure sharpness of detail and evenness of gray tones.

SYSTEM concerns the pattern of operation of a subject, in terms of its interdependent elements. The concept sketch represents a system pattern between a source and a terminal, which passes through two intermediate stations. Here, basic subject elements include the flow route and the four stations. The composition itself is built around an arrow convention, which gives it a symbolic context.

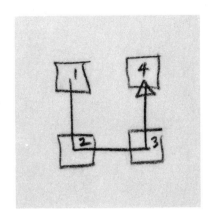

The aim of design is to produce a logical schematic diagram. Form vocabulary includes a solid linear flow form and station box shapes (represented in line so that the underlying flow form will be continuously visible). The flow form is shaded so as not to block out the boxes, and so that word forms can be seen on top of it. This means that spatial organization can be multi-plane. To assure this effect, superimposed forms are clearly differentiated both in structure and in non-alignment of edges. Relationship between the four boxes on the forward plane is achieved by similarity in size, shape, and edge alignment.

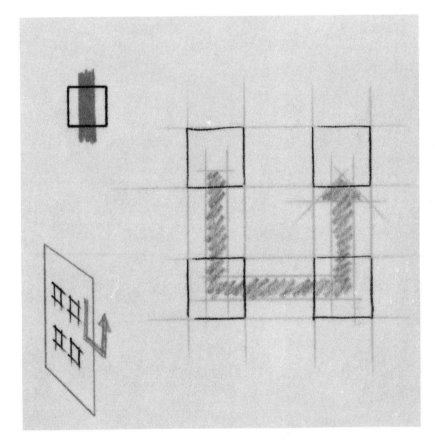

At a later stage, word meanings will be added to the figure model to identify its subject matter. Design has anticipated this need in its treatment of form sizes, and in its spacing. The execution of this figure will be with ink and acetate.

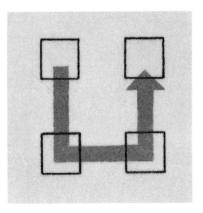

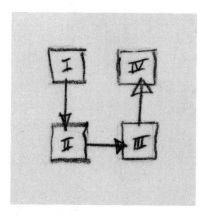

PROCESS concerns the procedure of independent subject actions, as a succession of related events. In this example, the concept shows a process which relates four separate subject phases. These phases constitute the primary elements. Since their directional links act as subordinate elements, the figure remains in an overall context that is abstract.

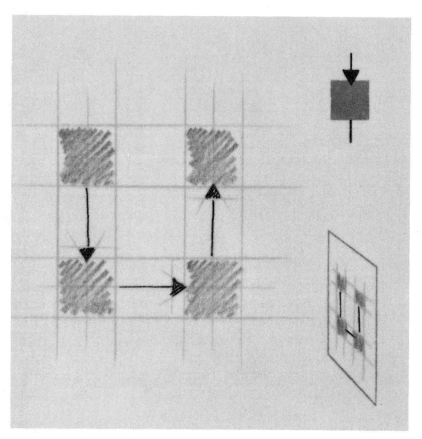

This design seeks to present a schematic arrangement. Its form vocabulary is simple, consisting of shaded phase-boxes and arrow-headed lines which connect them in consecutive fashion. Shape and line vocabulary serves to differentiate the two element classes, while members of each class are related by being identical. Through direct connection and consistent edge alignment, the entire figure rests on a single plane. This is done to maintain a sense of parallel meaning among the phase elements, and to keep the links in a dependent relation to the phase boxes. The boxes are solid for emphasis, and shaded so that identifying black lettering can be included within.

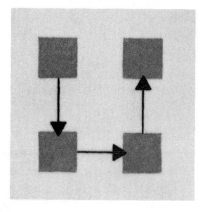

Again, design plans for the addition of word forms by allowing sufficient space in the shapes where they will be located. The media of execution will be ink and acetate, to achieve sharp line quality and the fine shade value required as a background for the lettering.

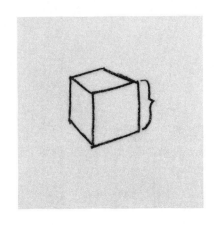

SIZE concerns the physical extent of a subject, in terms of the space it occupies. Here, the concept sketch indicates a size measurement of a cube object; specifically, its height. The primary elements of this figure are therefore the object and its measurement. The parts of the cube constitute secondary elements. The physical character of the cube places the figure in an objective context.

In this case, design aims at generalized representation. Line and shape are the vocabulary. The cube object is constructed within an angular perspective framework, and offset to the left to emphasize the plane to which the height bracket is attached. The height bracket itself is shaded as a shape, to differentiate it from the outline cube and to give it emphasis. The bracket edges are aligned with the cube edges in order to relate the measurement with the cube's height. The cube is shown only in black outline, since its physical surface features are not the concern of this figure.

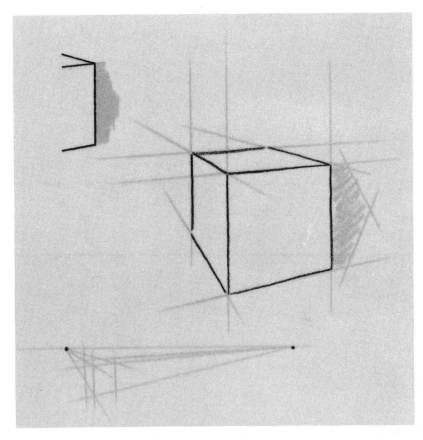

In the figure model, description of height will require the addition of numerical form to the pointed side of the bracket whose shape has been designed for this purpose. Execution will employ ink and acetate.

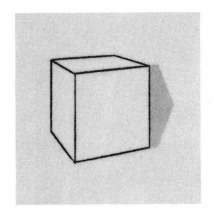

41

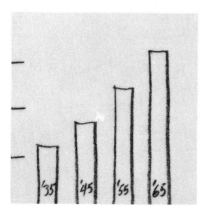

QUANTITY concerns the amount of a subject, in terms of a fixed scale of measure. The concept sketch shown here represents a comparison of quantities of a subject measured at time intervals. The four quantities, themselves, constitute the subject elements. A fixed scale of measurement acts as a frame of reference. To present a numerical abstraction, the figure assumes an abstract context.

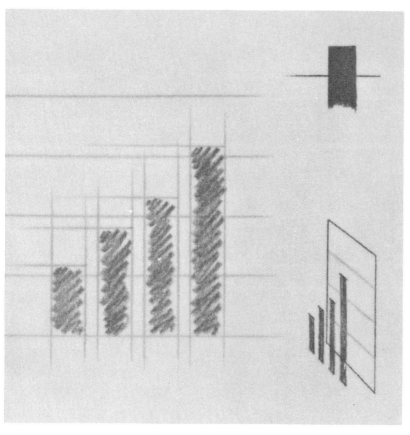

Here, design aims at comparative relation. The form vocabulary consists of line and shape. The shape bars are of uniform width, but measured in height (in relation to the scale of lines) to correspond with subject amounts. They are spaced close enough to enable visual comparison, but far enough apart to permit individual differentiation. Spatial organization is multiplane, automatically produced by the difference in width between the bars and the scale lines. This facilitates an easy reading of bar heights without scale interference. The entire figure is shaded to soften the visual impact of the bars.

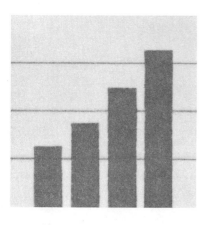

While identifying words and quantifying numbers will be necessary to complete the meaning of this figure model, they will be applied outside the image area and will, therefore, require no special design accommodations. As such, they will act as references to the bars and lines. This figure will be executed in ink and acetate.

TREND concerns the progressive increase or decrease of a subject, in terms of its amount. The concept shown here describes the increasing trend of a subject in terms of a coordinate scale. Trend is represented by a curve which generalizes a succession of numerical amounts. The curve and the coordinate scale (as a frame of reference) are the figurative elements. The context is necessarily abstract.

In this case, design acts to refine forms whose positions are otherwise determined by quantitative factors. The vocabulary is limited to point and line, the latter of which is varied in color value. The curve is emphasized as black, while the supporting grid is subordinated as a gray shade. This differentiates the curve and grid into a multi-plane spatial organization, reducing their visual interference to a minimum. Data points, representing numerical coordinate values drawn from subject data, are shown in black, and are integrated into the curve which generalizes their trend.

Here, again, to complete the meaning of the figure, identifying words and quantifying numbers will be applied outside the image area. Therefore, no design accommodations are required in the figure model. Ink alone will be the medium in which this figure will be executed.

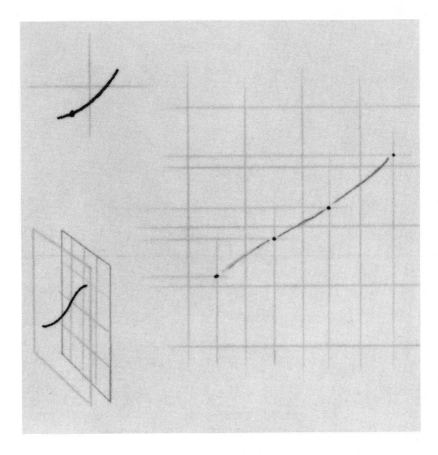

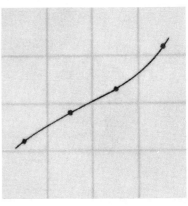

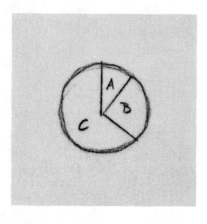

DIVISION concerns the separation of a whole amount in terms of its component quantities. In this example, the concept presents a subject amount which is divided into three component segments, their sizes varying in proportion to their percentage of the whole. Subject elements include the whole and its divisions. The showing of abstract percentage requires an abstract context.

The aim of design in this figure is to provide form which effectively represents the divided mass. The problem is not a difficult one, and is solved with a vocabulary of line and shape. The circular shape of the whole is shaded in value to allow black segment lines to be differentiated. Since the lines are related to the edges of the circular shape, the spatial organization of the figure remains plane. This is appropriate, inasmuch as the division lines must be seen to be in contact with the circular form to be meaningful.

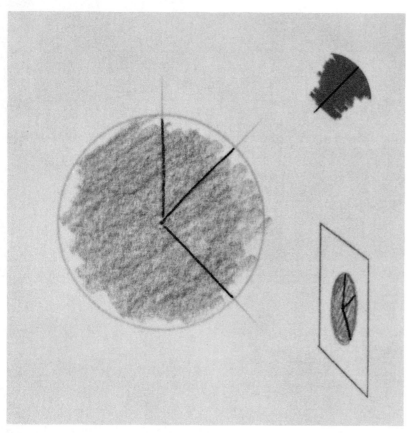

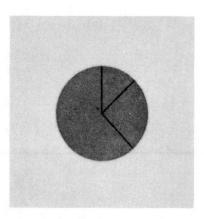

To complete the figure, identification will be added within each segment. Although this does not affect the essential design of the figure model, the size and position of these identifying forms will be a design consideration in itself. In execution, this figure will employ ink and acetate.

AREA concerns the space occupied by a subject in relation to its natural surroundings. This concept indicates the areas within a given environment where mountain ranges are situated. Here, subject elements are fluid, yet separated into two general areas of occurrence. Although flat in character, the geographic subject matter is presented within a context of objective reality.

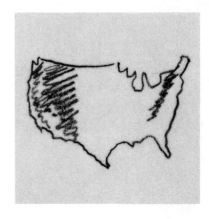

In this case, design aims at a physical representation of realities rarely seen as a whole, and uses artificial data (contour maps) to project physical features. The form vocabulary consists primarily of irregular shading, from light to dark, built up within the geographic shape of the subject area, and is supported outside by a linear environmental framework. The figure is plane in its spatial organization, but the geographic surface structure is represented in physical relief through the use of chiaroscuro. A single imaginary light source on the left provides the light and shadow cues which enable differentiation of the mountain formations.

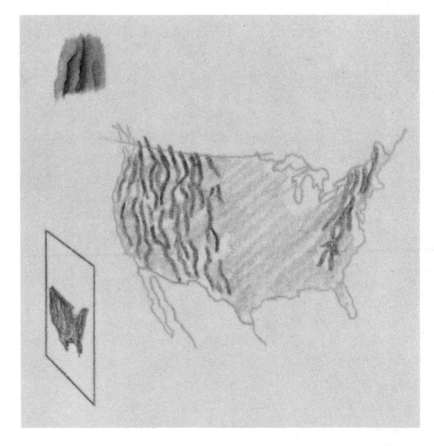

Three mountain areas, as basic elements, will require identification. Since the figure model's physical description of these areas allows little room for words, letter forms will have to be carefully placed. This figure will have to be executed in tempera, due to the detailed irregularity of its form.

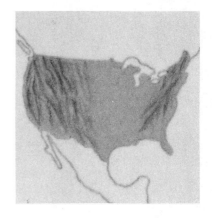

45

LOCATION concerns the spatial relationship between a subject and its overall environment. In this case the subject presented by the concept sketch consists of many specific locations within a geographic frame of reference. The locations constitute multiple subject elements. Since the subject locations and the geography are abbreviated forms of reality, the context is considered to be symbolic.

Here, design seeks to present a map image. The form vocabulary employed is a simple one, consisting of points and irregular lines. The points are emphasized as black, and differentiated from the geography by representing the geographic outline in gray shade. This creates a multi-plane spatial organization which provides a subtle separation between the point elements and the linear framework. To achieve accurate locations, the preliminary design builds on a map with political subdivisions for reference. These subdivisions are omitted in the final design since they are not essential to the pattern of locations and tend to confuse the image.

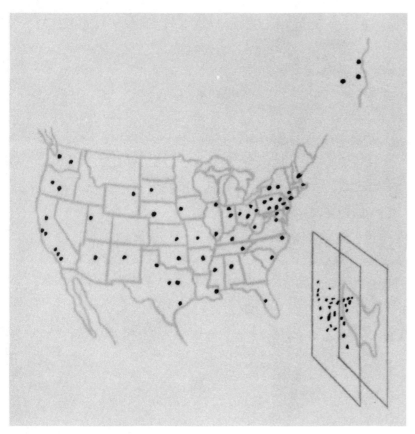

This figure model will not require internal identification. However, a key for the explanation of point elements will be included in one of the open corners of the figure. The medium of execution will be ink.

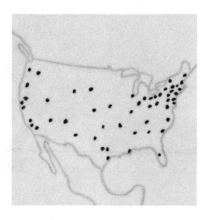

POSITION concerns the spatial relation of a subject element to other elements within an area. Here, the concept describes a grouping of positions within an area that is structured by a street network. The four positions and the network constitute the subject elements of this figure. The reduction of real objects and places to generalized forms puts the figure in a symbolic context.

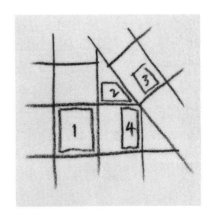

In this example, design aims at diagrammatic representation. Here, shape and linear form constitute the vocabulary. The important block positions are emphasized as black, and differentiated from the street network by showing the latter as gray shade. While this vocabulary technically produces a multi-plane spatial organization, the separation of black and gray elements tends to be ambiguous, due to the confinement of the blocks in the network. This is appropriate, however, since the blocks have meaning both as physical members in the network and as detached position elements.

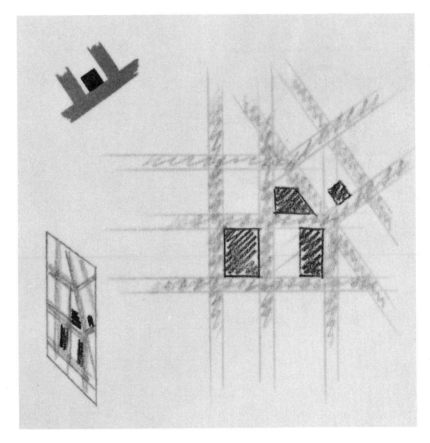

Identification of relevant blocks and streets will be required to complete the meaning of the figure. Space for this has been allowed in the design of the figure model, although block numbers will require reversal (as white). Acetate will be used for the execution of the figure.

47

The eye's lens is located in back of the iris and held there with suspensory ligaments. Contraction of the muscles which are attached on them causes the lens lens to become more of a spherical shape.

is

be

to

in

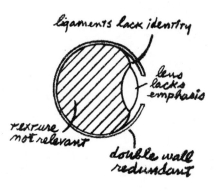

ligaments lack identity

lens lacks emphasis

texture not relevant

double wall redundant

ERRORS IN: LANGUAGE

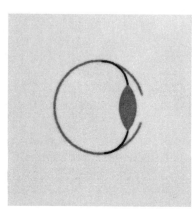

STATEMENT

ECONOMY

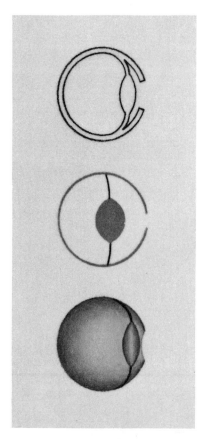

3
VISUAL EDITING

A misspelled word is always confusing, and often misunderstood. A form, also, may be "misspelled" with respect to its visual meaning. In reviewing a text, an editor will correct such misspelling, as well as errors in vocabulary, grammar, and syntax. He will examine the form of the statement to assess its effectiveness in conveying the intended idea. Since the graphic figure can also be faulty in its form, it, too, requires editing prior to production. A weak form vocabulary may make the figure visually inarticulate. Spatial contradictions may render it ambiguous. Its elements may be incorrectly translated, or it may not focus upon the intended idea. Its form may be awkward, or its identification confused. Moreover, it may not be economical to produce. Therefore, without visual editing, the figure may be difficult to "read", inaccurate in its meaning, or wasteful in its execution. To avoid such problems, the figure design must be critically evaluated for possible errors in *language, statement,* and *economy.* In each case, the recognition of error is less important only than its correction. The following pages illustrate some of the errors which might have occurred in the design of the figure examples previously considered. Problems concerning word and number elements are omitted here, but will be examined in the next section.

LANGUAGE errors affect the form of the graphic figure. They can inhibit its quality of expression, its clarity, and its unity. If the figure is to communicate visually, it must be designed for the eye. It must be articulate in its vocabulary and logical in its spatial grammar. It must integrate the elements of the figure into a coherent and readable image. Here, visual esthetics perform a practical role.

The first figure suffers the defect of being ambiguous in its structure, which produces an optical reversal of its apparent form and makes it difficult to comprehend. It lacks correct vocabulary and perspective structure (see page 36).

The second figure exhibits an excessive use of line vocabulary which creates visual monotony rather than a clear differentiation of line and shape elements. Also, arbitrary spacing causes awkward isolation at the top and crowdedness at the bottom (see page 37).

The third figure fails to show its arrows with decisive form, and, therefore, makes them difficult to read as symbols. This malformation could be corrected by using solid, triangular shapes (see page 40).

The fourth figure is confused by a visual interference of the grid lines with the trend line. Since the grid is simply a frame of reference, it should be visually subordinated so that the trend curve can be clearly distinguished (see page 43).

AMBIGUOUS
STRUCTURE

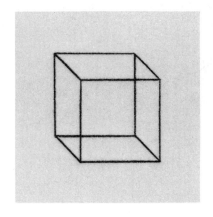

MONOTONOUS
VOCABULARY

AND

AWKWARD
SPACING

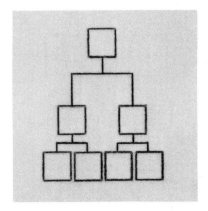

MALFORMED
ARROW SYMBOLS

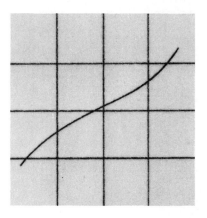

CURVE AND GRID
INTERFERENCE

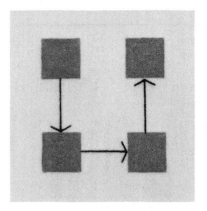

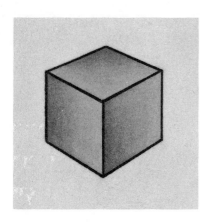

SUPERFLUOUS
OUTLINE

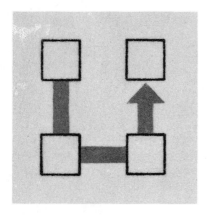

DISCONTINUITY
OF FLOW

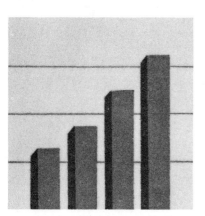

CONTRADICTION
OF CONTEXT

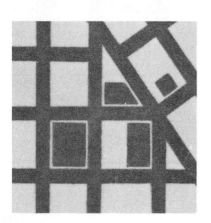

CONFUSION
OF ELEMENTS

STATEMENT errors concern mistakes in the form of the figure which primarily affect its meaning. Such forms may be visually consistent, or even expressive. The problem here is that they tend to express the wrong idea. In graphic communication, form acts in the service of the idea. It must, therefore, act correctly, or it may distort the figure into a visual lie.

The first figure dramatizes the box image by giving it a heavy black outline. Impressive as it may seem, the outline is, nevertheless, shown in a context of physical reality and, therefore, appears as a wire frame around the box. It is misleading and superfluous to the essential idea (see page 35).

The second figure cuts up the flow line and fits its parts neatly between station elements. While this produces a cleaner image, it also breaks the essential continuity of the system and destroys the logic of the figure (see page 39).

The third figure contradicts the abstract context through which it presents quantitative information, by representing the quantities as physical structures. Here, solid form is both meaningless and misleading (see page 42).

The fourth figure confuses block and street elements by representing them with identical shade values. Since their structures coincide so closely, they require differentiation in color value to avoid misunderstanding (see page 47).

ECONOMY in the figure may be defined as a maximum of expression with a minimum of expenditure. Economy constraints are not intended to imprison design, but rather to define the boundaries of necessity within which it can perform usefully. Since too much form can be an obstacle in the way of seeing the idea, visual economy in the selection and treatment of form is always desirable. Practical economy, as well, must be considered in the design of the figure, since too much form can also be an expensive luxury.

The first figure pictorializes an entire street environment, despite the fact that it is irrelevant to the communicative aim—the bus movement pattern. Here, less would mean more (see page 38).

The second figure unnecessarily describes the surface quality of a cube object, when only its height is required. Refinement of the height bracket rather than the cube surface would have produced a more efficient figure (see page 41).

The third figure not only describes the physical surface intended, but exceeds that area in its total description. A simple outline of adjacent geography would have served the purpose (see page 45).

The fourth figure is crowded with many details which are not essential to its purpose, which is to show city locations. Clarity as well as efficiency would have been served by a more economical approach (see page 46).

IRRELEVANT ENVIRONMENT

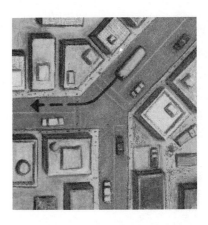

UNNECESSARY REFINEMENT

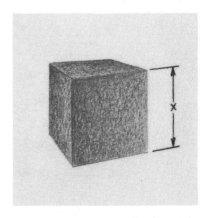

EXCESSIVE DESCRIPTION

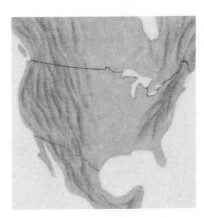

NON-ESSENTIAL INFORMATION

4

IMAGE MEANING

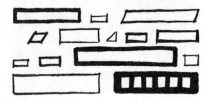

WORDS and NUMBERS AS PART of THE IMAGE ARE ALSO SUBJECT TO VISUAL DESIGN

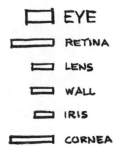

▭	EYE
▭	RETINA
▭	LENS
▭	WALL
▭	IRIS
▭	CORNEA

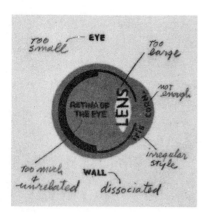

CONTENT

PLACEMENT

CHARACTER

Words and numbers, as part of the image, are also subject to visual design. Since they are seen as well as read, how they appear in the figure is no less important than what they say. Their purpose is to augment the meaning of those elements of the figure which require identification or quantification in order to be understood; therefore, they serve to complete the image as a graphic statement. For that reason, the figure should be designed to accommodate necessary words and numbers, which, in turn, should be seen as participating blocks of form and designed in relation to the form of the figure. Since the overall purpose of the figure is to visualize ideas, words and numbers should be appropriately subordinated to what is shown. They should simply identify and quantify the figure, not restate it. Without careful design, words and numbers can spoil the sense of the figure. They can tell too much or not enough. They can be too large or too small. They can appear unrelated, or dissociated. Their style can be irregular, when instead it should match the regularity of the image elements. Therefore, the effectiveness of words and numbers depends not only on the quality of their *content,* but also upon their *placement* and *character.* The following figure examples serve to illustrate the role of these factors.

CONTENT concerns the idea substance embodied in words or numbers. In the graphic figure such content necessarily applies to specific visual form, and serves to attach meaning to that form. For this reason, words and numbers need to make sense only in terms of what is shown, saying neither more nor less than is required to identify or quantify the image and complete the idea. Therefore, content itself should be "designed", in order to convey meaning to the figure without confusing or obstructing its visual sense.

The first figure identifies the idea-boxes in its organization, but omits from their labels those words whose meanings are visually apparent.

The second figure also identifies idea-boxes; this time, to convey process. Their phase character is visually apparent, so only individual numerals are required.

The third figure must interpret its subject data to produce appropriate numbers with which to quantify the image scale. Ordinate and abscissa definitions derive directly from the table.

The fourth figure shows most of the idea visually, and requires only a detached key for uniform identification and quantification of point symbols.

SUBJECT X
ELEMENT A
PART 1
PART 2
ELEMENT B
PART 1
PART 2

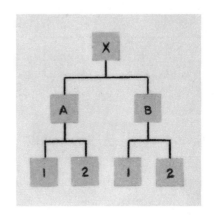

PHASE I
PHASE II
PHASE III
PHASE IV

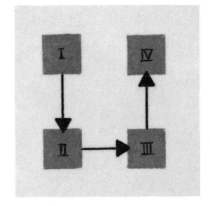

YR.	AMT.
'35	12
'45	18
'55	23
'65	32

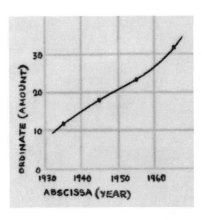

...CITIES OF THE U.S. WITH A POPULATION OVER 100,000...

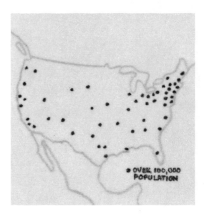

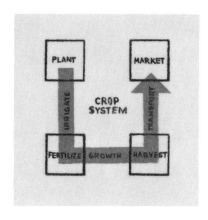

CROP SYSTEM
   PLANT
   FERTILIZE
   HARVEST
   MARKET
   +
   IRRIGATE
   GROWTH
   TRANSPORT

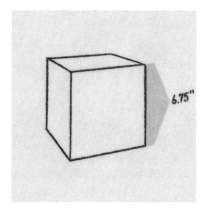

HEIGHT OF BOX:
6.75"

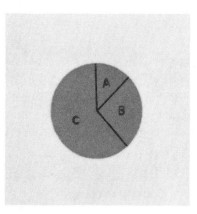

PART	%
A	13
B	25
C	62
TOTAL	100

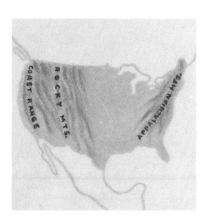

ROCKY MTS.

COAST RANGE

APPALACHIAN MTS.

PLACEMENT concerns the spatial position of words or numbers with respect to visual elements in the figure. To operate effectively, a word or number element should be clearly related to the visual element it describes, while at the same time remaining independent of neighboring forms. In effect, word and number elements are conceived to act jointly with their associated form elements, and should be positioned to produce this interaction in a way that contributes to the communicative purpose. Effective placement can be achieved through proximity, alignment, separate reference, centering, and conformity.

The first figure relates identifying words to visual elements through centered placement and alignment with form edges.

The second figure employs a separate reference form (shaded bracket) whose point determines the placement of the quantifying number, which is angled to echo the perspective structure.

The third figure relates identifying letters to its segments by placing each letter in the physical center of its segment.

The fourth figure associates word meanings with form elements by curving the word structures so that their directions conform with the form features they identify.

CHARACTER concerns the physical structure of words or numbers with respect to their symbolic function in the image. The exact nature of this character depends on what form elements they relate to, what they mean, and what they do. Many variations in character are possible. Generally, *sans serif* styles (as in this text) tend to be most compatible to the character of visual form since their structure is formalized rather than elaborated. Size, angularity, spacing, weight, and color value are major variables in designing the character of word and number elements.

The first figure demonstrates a use of large and small size, and upper and lower case style to create dominant and subordinate title elements.

The second figure uses words which are straight, slanted, condensed, or extended to visually characterize the nature of their various meanings.

The third figure employs bold and light number forms to emphasize bar identities and subordinate the grid quantification.

The fourth figure reverses (to white on black) the numerical identification of its major elements to clearly differentiate them from the street labels, and to permit the block elements to remain emphasized as black.

INTERIOR VIEW OF BOX

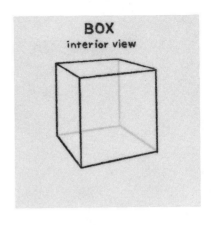

MOVEMENT PATTERN OF BUS FROM HIGHWAY TO ROAD

YR.	AMT.
'35	12
'45	18
'55	23
'65	32

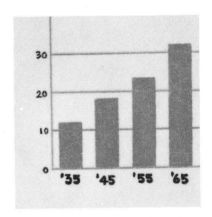

1. 233 CENTRAL ST.
2. 1704 4TH ST.
3. 1836 4TH ST.
4. 1797 5TH ST.

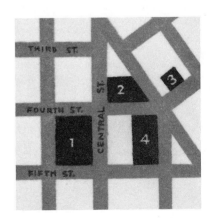

ILLUSTRATION

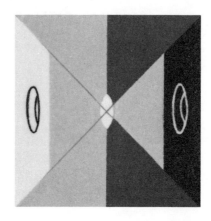

PHOTOGRAPHY

PLATEMAKING

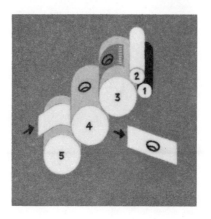

PRINTING

THE GRAPHIC VOICE

In the broadest sense, design goes beyond the drawing board. If the figure is to be reproduced, both designer and illustrator must consider the process, and see the figure with a "graphic eye". Using the design model as a guide, illustration proceeds with the preparation of a working layout and the execution of the figure itself. The medium of execution varies in relation to the form of the figure and the reproduction process to be used. While many graphic processes exist, quality and efficiency generally find their best meeting in offset lithography. The steps in this process include photography, platemaking, and printing. In photography, a film negative of the illustration material is made. This negative is placed between a sensitized plate and a light source, which "burns" the areas of the plate exposed by the negative. In printing, ink (1) and water (2) are rolled onto the plate cylinder (3). The "burned" areas of the plate accept ink and reject water, while the rest of the plate accepts a water coating which inhibits inking. The plate image is transferred, or "offset" onto the "blanket" cylinder (4), which prints the image on paper moving between the blanket and the roller (5). In reproduction, as in illustration, exact procedure is determined by the nature of the figure. In production terms, the graphic figure can be *simple, compound,* or *complex.*

56

SIMPLE figures are those in which a plate is burned, by using a single negative made from illustration material prepared on a single page. This is the most economical of procedures for reproduction. While its usual material is line work, broad dot-patterns on acetate sheets can be included. In some cases, a "screen" (a fine dot-pattern negative) is superimposed over the negative to create a uniform shade figure.

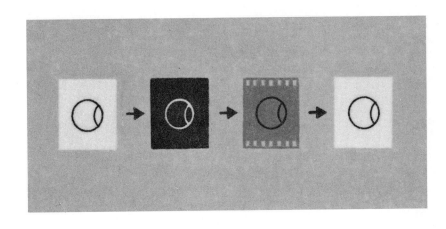

The first figure is executed in ink, since that medium lends itself best to the construction of solid and dotted lines. A variety of tools are used with the ink medium, including pens of varying sizes, templates, triangles, curves, etc. A description of techniques, however, will not be attempted here.

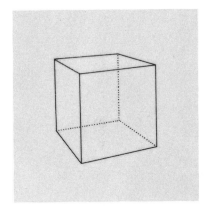

INK

The second figure is also executed in ink, but an acetate shade (dot-pattern) form is cut out and added to represent the bracket shape. Pre-printed dot-patterns on acetate are generally too rough to permit superimposed lettering, but since no lettering is required here, production efficiency makes this the best method.

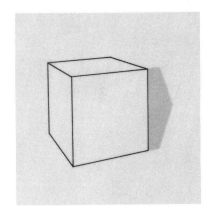

INK + ACETATE SHADE

The third figure is executed in ink and solid acetate. A fine dot-pattern screen is used with the negative to produce a totally gray figure. Forms can be cut out of acetate sheets with a small knife. The color or pattern is printed on the top, and the back contains a wax adhesive so that forms can be burnished firmly into place on the page.

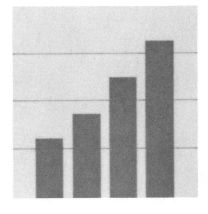

INK + SOLID ACETATE (SCREENED)

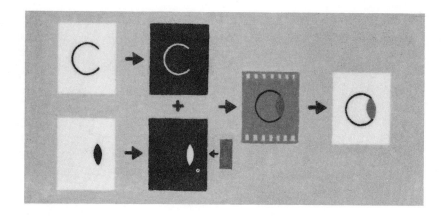

COMPOUND figures are those in which a plate is double-burned, using two negatives made from illustration material prepared on two separate pages. This is done when the figure requires a fine-quality shade in conjunction with black form. The form to be shaded is executed solid on the second page, and a screen is added to its negative. The plate is then burned twice, using each negative, to form the composite image.

The first figure is executed on two pages. Since the form is line, ink is used for both. One page component contains the curve line, and the other contains the grid whose negative is screened prior to platemaking.

INK
(SCREENED GRID)

The second figure is executed in acetate, again on two page components. Here, the form is more easily cut out of acetate than constructed in ink. The network component is screened, while the block pattern is burned black.

SOLID ACETATE
(SCREENED NETWORK)

The third figure is executed in both ink and acetate. While ink lends itself best to the line component, acetate is the best medium for the flow form, which is screened.

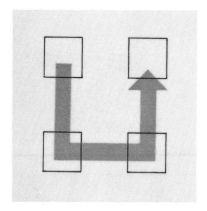

INK + SOLID ACETATE
(SCREENED FLOW)

COMPLEX figures are those in which a plate is burned, using a single negative that has been "halftoned." Here, the illustration material is on a single page, but due to its complications of shading a halftone screen (not to be confused with a screen negative) must be used to translate its form into reproducible dot-patterns. In practice, halftone processing requires particular care and makes the photography step a demanding one.

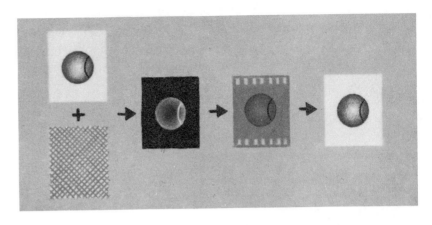

The first figure is executed in ink and acetate. Since two additional shades are used with black, economy favors halftoning over triple-burning, and the figure is prepared on a single page. In this case, gray shades are represented directly on the page using continuous tone acetate grays.

INK + GRAY ACETATE

The second figure is executed in tempera, due to the detailed variations of its shading. Brush technique is important here. In this figure, alternative media, such as designers' colors, gouache, or liquid acrylics could be used. This figure, too, is halftoned.

TEMPERA

The third figure is executed in airbrush, since that medium lends itself best to the kind of even shading required by the cube figure. In execution, sharp edges are obtained by masking off each plane of the cube in turn, and spraying the interior to completion.

AIRBRUSH

59

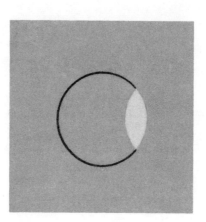

IV

TO SHOW *WHAT*

What something is concerns its natural appearance, physical structure, or organization of parts in relation to the whole. It is clear that these three aspects are related in meaning. Appearance can mean the organization of reality as an image, structure can mean internal appearance, and organization can mean abstract structure. Yet, it is also clear that each of these aspects suggests a somewhat different focus on ideas, and presents a unique view in terms of showing *what* something is. Since the possibility of different views allows a wider range of communicative alternatives, appearance, structure, and organization will be considered here in terms of their separate capabilities, and explored as primary problem areas.

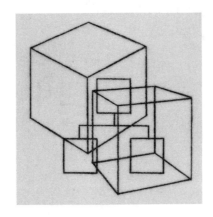

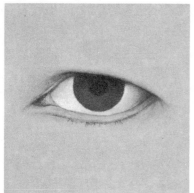

1
APPEARANCE

PHYSICAL

FORMALIZED

SURFACE

ENVIRONMENTAL

TRANSPARENT

COMPOSITIONAL

Appearance concerns the natural features of a subject as they are seen by the eye under normal circumstances. In the graphic figure, these natural features can be shown directly in terms of their *physical* appearance, or *formalized* to emphasize essential aspects. *Surface* qualities can be described in detail, if required, or the subject can be shown in relation to its *environmental* features. *Transparent* subjects can also be described, as well as the *compositional* appearance of subject elements. The following figure models represent design solutions to specific problems in these areas.

PHYSICAL appearance shows the natural features of a subject as a visual illusion. Perspective spatial organization, the action of light and shadow, and detailed visual description are important factors in creating a realistic image. Obstructive or unnecessary subject matter elements (such as background) can often be omitted to clarify the basic physical features.

FIGURE 1. A simple cube object shown in angular perspective to emphasize volumetric mass (see page 35).

FIGURE 2. A box in which specific details are emphasized, based on the structure of the cube of figure 1.

FIGURE 3. A biological form in which shape subtleties are suggested through varied surface description.

FIGURE 4. A biological neuron cell showing a wide variety of form details.

FIGURE 5. A gas reduction regulator whose volumetric form is described by the shading of curved surfaces within an angular perspective framework.

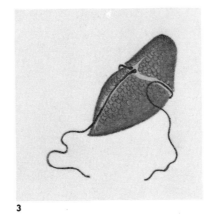
1

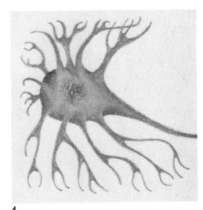
2

3

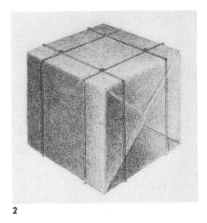
4

5

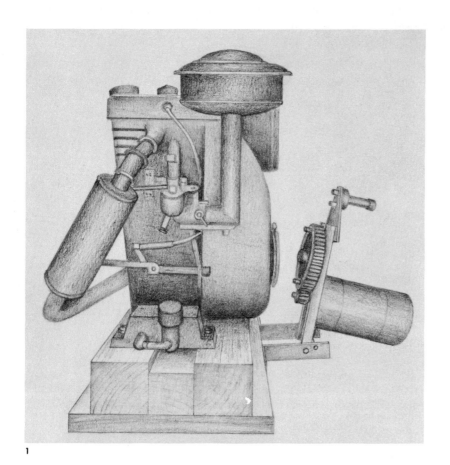

1

PHYSICAL appearance (continued)

FIGURE 1. A machine shown in parallel perspective, to permit a view of certain parts which occur on one particular side.

FIGURE 2. A boiler, in which cylindrical form shading is shown in conjunction with fine detail description.

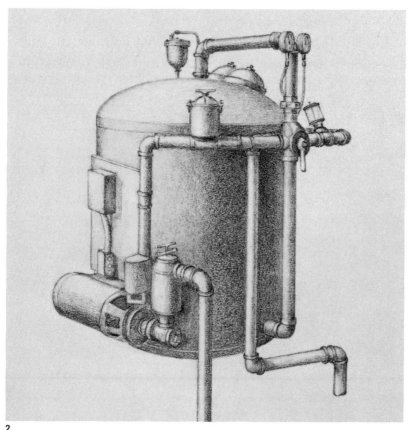

2

FORMALIZED appearance shows the subject in an objective context in which natural features are modified or replaced with simpler forms to give sharper definition to essential aspects. Here, clarity is enhanced at the expense of visual reality.

FIGURE 1. A simple cube in which the shading effect of light is formalized to differentiate its physical planes.

FIGURE 2. The same cube shown in a different perspective position to emphasize its frontal plane.

FIGURE 3. The same cube with frontal plane removed to show its interior—insofar as it can normally be seen.

FIGURE 4. Light bulbs whose outside form is generalized for subordination to detailed internal description.

FIGURE 5. A biological fossil whose form is generalized in the absence of actual subject matter.

FIGURE 6. A multicellular organism showing dominant and subordinate cell forms.

FIGURE 7. Various work vehicles represented in silhouette form for identification purposes.

1

2

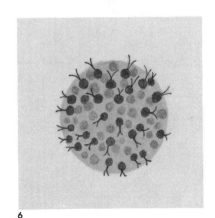

3

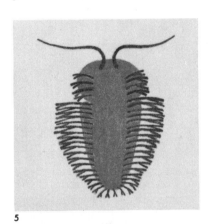

4

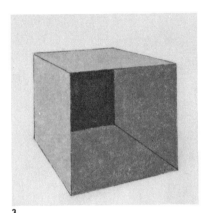

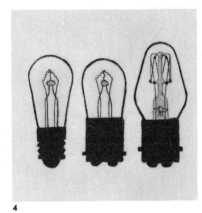

5

6

7

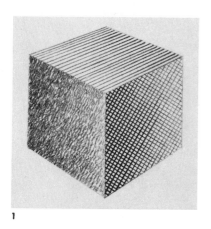
1

2

SURFACE appearance can be shown through emphatic description of the physical textures and patterns which give the subject its tactile character. While surface appearance is an aspect of physical appearance, shading and specific details tend to be subordinated to overall textural quality.

FIGURE 1. Textured planes on a simple cube.

FIGURE 2. A metallic connector, showing different varieties of machine-made surface form.

FIGURE 3. A bird whose feathered surface is shown by subtle variations in a single, continuous texture.

FIGURE 4. A panoramic view of a locale in which specific details are subordinated to a surface pattern impression of the whole.

3

4

ENVIRONMENTAL appearance presents the subject in the context of its natural surroundings, showing these surroundings to the degree that they are necessary to the sense of the subject. To maintain subject emphasis, however, environmental features are visually subordinated.

FIGURE 1. A simple cube shown in relation to surrounding cubes which are simplified as outline form.

FIGURE 2. A distributor shown in its natural relation to other mechanical parts which are subdued to a neutral value for subordination.

FIGURE 3. A piston mechanism emphasized as black in an environment of gray forms.

FIGURE 4. Here, the body surface of a bug, where a hairlike receptor is shown as the subject, constitutes the environment.

FIGURE 5. A space vehicle brought spatially forward by its lighter shading against a dark receding environment. The earth form acts as a spatially intermediate, secondary element.

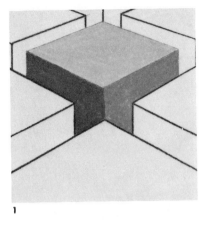

1

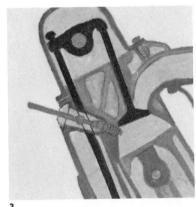

2

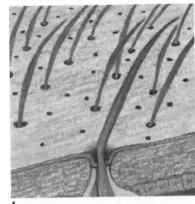

3

4

5

1

2

3

ENVIRONMENTAL appearance (continued).

FIGURE 1. A speedometer shown within a subdued gray car interior.

FIGURE 2. A white container and its associated mechanism emphasized against a dark environment.

FIGURE 3. A regulator, fully described, connected to a gas tank whose shade description is lightened to subordinate it as an environmental element.

TRANSPARENT appearance can be shown by subtle shading, which describes the edges of the transparent form but leaves its body relatively open. The presence of solid form behind the transparent substance adds a further cue to the illusion of transparency.

FIGURE 1. A simple cube in which edge lines of interior corners suggest transparency.

FIGURE 2. The same cube encasing a ball that allows on the front surface of the cube a visible reflection to heighten the sense of transparency.

FIGURE 3. A radio tube whose transparency is suggested by graduated shading which fades into an open center.

FIGURE 4. An enlarged insect whose wings appear transparent due to the faint description of legs and body underneath.

1

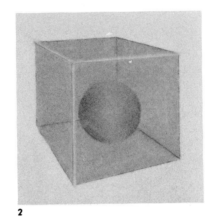

2

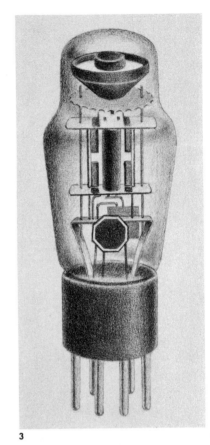

3

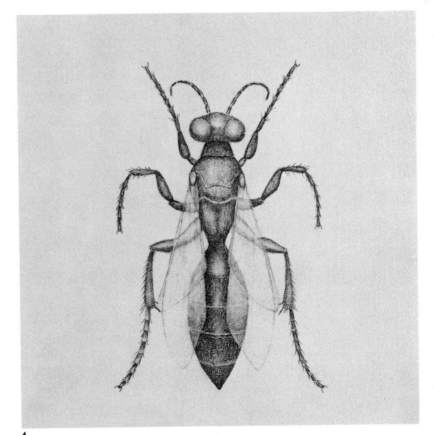

4

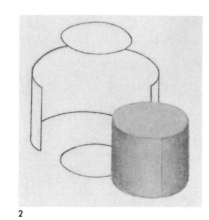

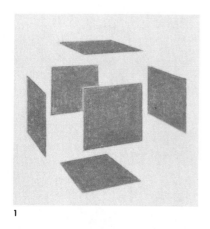

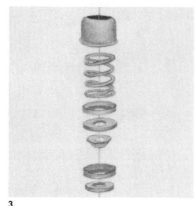

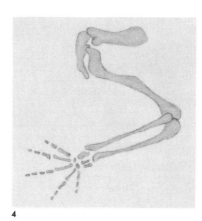

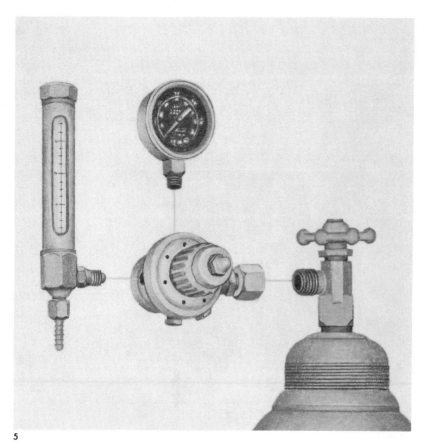

COMPOSITIONAL appearance shows the constituent elements of a subject in terms of their physical features and their functional relationships to one another. Components are related to the whole through position and alignment.

FIGURE 1. A disassembled cube whose composition is suggested by the spatial placement of components in direct relation to their positions in the cube.

FIGURE 2. A cylinder with a secondary representation (subordinated in outline) of its compositional elements.

FIGURE 3. A grouping of spring components related by a faint guideline in the center.

FIGURE 4. The forelimb skeleton of a reptile related by visual continuity alone.

FIGURE 5. A regulator, two gauges, and a tank are described individually and related as a functional system through the use of connecting guidelines.

COMPOSITIONAL appearance (continued).

FIGURE 1. An electronic unit whose component elements are related to the whole by guidelines which indicate the places where parts interconnect.

FIGURE 2. A trombone disassembled along center lines and related by guidelines. This type of representation is sometimes referred to as an "exploded" view.

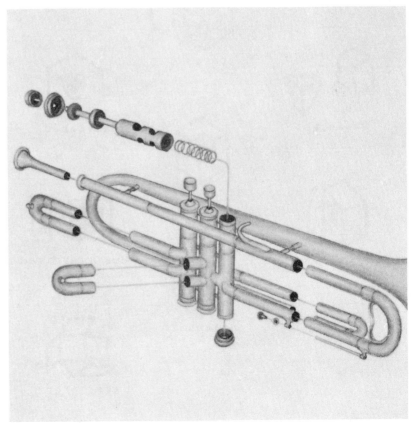

1

2

2
STRUCTURE

EXTERIOR

INVISIBLE

INTERNAL

INTERIOR

COMPOUND

ENLARGED

REVEALED

SEMI-SECTION

SECTION

SEGMENT

MULTI-SECTION

SEPARATED

Structure concerns the essential physical constitution of a subject, beyond what can normally be seen. In the graphic figure, normally hidden aspects of the subject's *exterior* can be represented, or inner elements can be shown in a subject whose outward features are treated as *invisible.* By altering external appearances the entire structural character of the *interior* can be shown, as well as other *internal* form features which are independent of the surrounding framework. *Compound* subject elements or *enlarged* subject details can be represented. If a random portion of the subject's surface form is removed, a *revealed* view of the structure within can be obtained. A *semi-section* cut into the subject can expose an area of the inner structural substance, and a *section* cut can expose an entire plane of inner structure. Moreover, a *multi-section* cut can enable two or more planes of structure to be shown in relation to each other, or a sectional *segment* can be removed from the subject to show a specific piece of its structural substance. Lastly, to show structure, the subject can be physically *separated* into its component elements. The following figure models represent design solutions to specific problems in these areas.

72

EXTERIOR structure can be shown by omitting form characteristics associated with surface planes of the subject, and representing its physical edges and corners, or those features which serve to identify its outlying boundaries. In this way, exterior aspects which are normally hidden can be shown within a unified skeletal framework.

FIGURE 1. A simple cube shown as an outline skeleton with subordinated gray lines to indicate hidden edges. Angular perspective is off-center to avoid line interference (see page 36).

FIGURE 2. The same cube using an expanded vocabulary to convey a sense of the cube's volume as well as its exterior skeleton of edges.

FIGURE 3. Farm machinery in which linear forms are treated as though they were transparent to maintain structural continuity.

FIGURE 4. A regulator employing the form vocabulary of figure 1 in a more complex manner to describe cylindrical features.

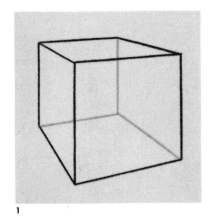
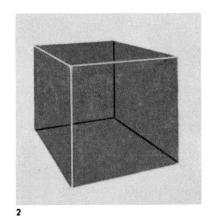

1

2

3

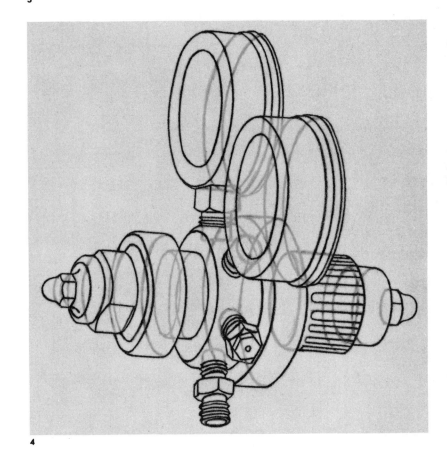

4

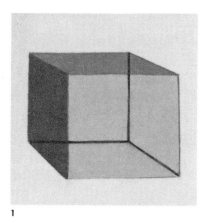

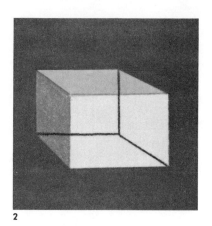

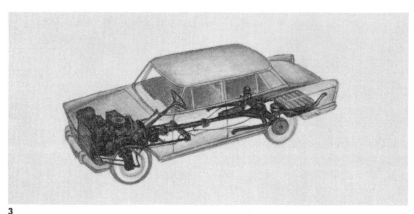

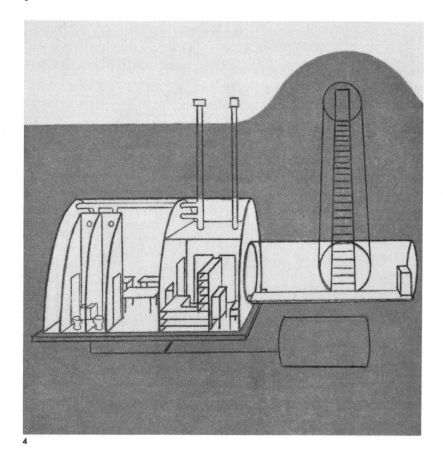

INVISIBLE structure is outer form which permits an inner view, while maintaining a sense of the subject's natural appearance. This means that the subject's outer shell or surface is treated as semi-transparent, to reveal certain physical elements within its body.

FIGURE 1. Interior corners within a formalized cube whose external surfaces are described by shaded planes.

FIGURE 2. A shift in the shade pattern of figure 1, creating a dark ground which permits an emphatic white frontal plane.

FIGURE 3. Mechanical elements inside a car whose body is otherwise described in terms of its physical appearance. This type of description is frequently called a "phantom" view.

FIGURE 4. An underground structure represented as a skeletal framework within a formalized section of earth which constitutes the outer form.

INVISIBLE structure (continued).

FIGURE 1. A tube of insulated wires in which successive layers of inner form are shown.

FIGURE 2. An object in which inner form emerges from its container to act as external form.

FIGURE 3. A human skeleton formalized as a shape structure within a subordinated outer body.

FIGURE 4. A carrot physically described within a section of earth as the outer form.

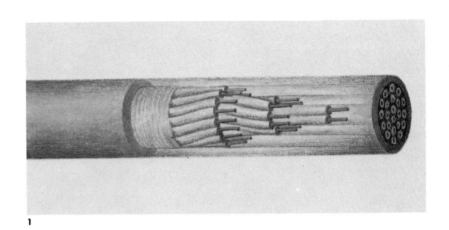

1

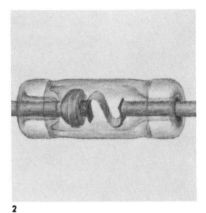

2

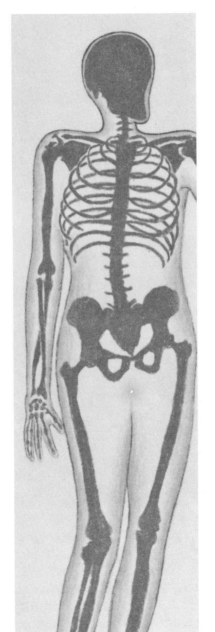

3

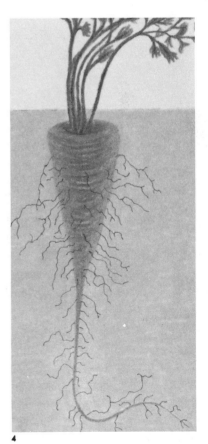

4

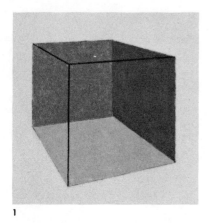

1

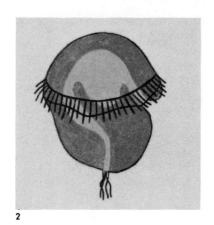

2

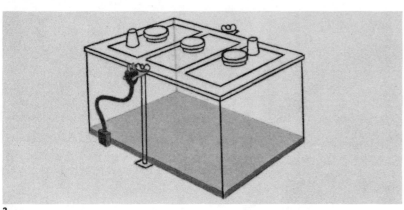

3

4

INTERIOR structure can be shown in its entirety by replacing the subject's outer shell with a linear skeleton that merely indicates its form. This permits a full description of interior features associated with the shell, in terms of their natural appearance.

FIGURE 1. The interior of a simple cube, formalized in its appearance.

FIGURE 2. A biological form (mollusk larva) whose interior structure is formalized for clarity.

FIGURE 3. A battery in which the interior floor structure is described, as well as the exterior plug associated with it.

FIGURE 4. An automobile interior which shows sectional structure cuts as well as inner surfaces.

INTERNAL structure shows subject elements which are inside but otherwise physically independent of the surrounding shell. Again, the subject's exterior is replaced with a simple framework which permits a full view of internal elements.

FIGURE 1. A formalized cube within a larger cube which is subordinated as an exterior skeleton.

FIGURE 2. A form reversal of figure 1 to lend body to the larger cube and emphasize the frontal plane of the smaller.

FIGURE 3. The circulatory system of an earthworm in which hidden edges of the exterior form are omitted for visual clarity.

FIGURE 4. The mechanical components of a radar tower whose internal positions are represented by shaded silhouettes. Guidelines relate the shaded forms to external descriptions of the elements, which are shown in terms of their compositional arrangement.

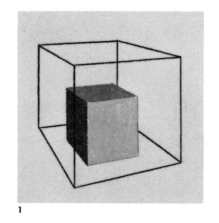
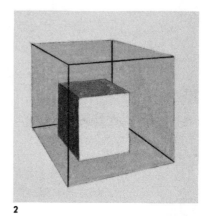

1

2

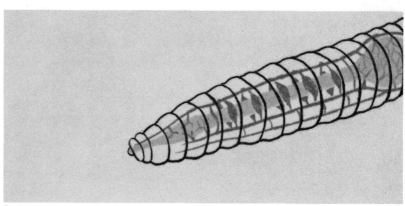

3

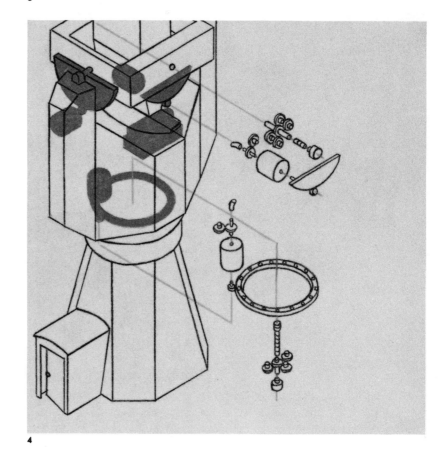

4

1

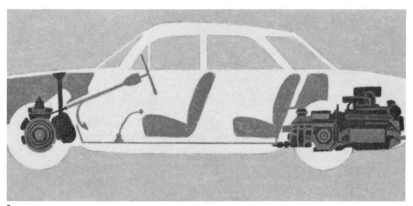

2

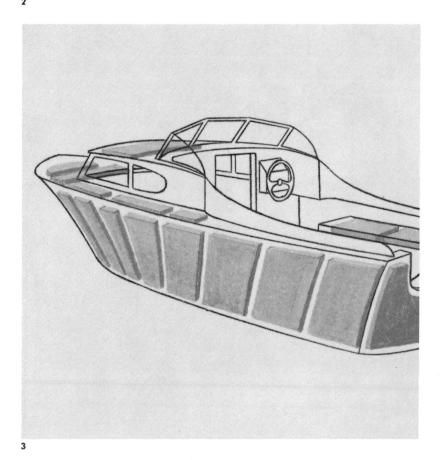

3

INTERNAL structure (continued).

FIGURE 1. Internal elements of an automobile, described in detail. For subject continuity, the external wheels are included as an integral part of the inner form structure.

FIGURE 2. Internal elements of an automobile, formalized in a side view for clarity. The surrounding structure is presented as a negative (white) shape, to lend body to the external form while providing adequate contrast for the shaded forms within.

FIGURE 3. Elements inside a boat, located in close relation to exterior planes rather than deep in the interior. Light shading is used to avoid confusion with the linear framework.

COMPOUND structure shows otherwise independent subject elements in a combined arrangement where they are visually differentiated, yet related with coinciding form features to represent the subject as an integrated whole.

FIGURE 1. Two simple cube elements in which one, as a drawer, appears to be partially occupying the other.

FIGURE 2. Two elements of a machine part shown with a complimentary vocabulary of line and shape.

FIGURE 3. A nephron (from a human body) in which system components are differentiated with light and dark shade.

FIGURE 4. An elevated railway using linear and shaded form to describe as well as differentiate the compound elements of the subject.

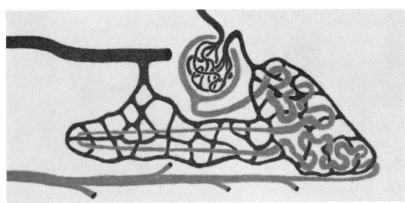

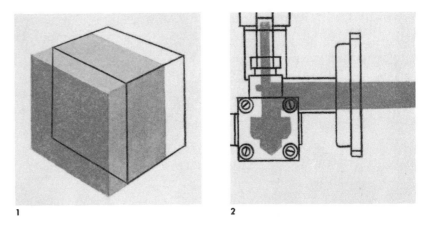

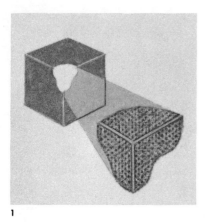

1

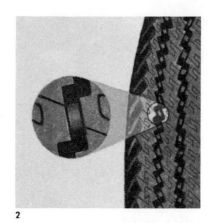

2

3

4

ENLARGED structure shows subject details which are too small to be represented in the same scale as the subject, but which are essential to a structural description of the subject. The enlargement is shown independently, but is related to the area of the subject which it represents.

FIGURE 1. A corner of a simple cube enlarged to show surface texture.

FIGURE 2. An enlargement of a tire tread detail which represents a typical unit of its entire structure.

FIGURE 3. The circulatory system of a squid whose enlargement is related to an internal view of the squid form.

FIGURE 4. A regulator gauge enlarged to show the exact calibration of its scale.

REVEALED structure is that which becomes visible by the imaginary removal of a portion of the subject's outer wall. The area of removal is described by an irregular edge, representing a physical cut into the surface of the subject's form. Therefore, this view is often referred to as a "cutaway". While the cut edge appears random in character, it is in fact designed to reveal certain specific features within the subject, while maintaining a sense of the subject's outer form continuity.

FIGURE 1. An arbitrary removal of a corner portion of a cube, to reveal the structure of its wall.

FIGURE 2. The interior structure of another cube, revealed by a wider opening.

FIGURE 3. The engine and steering mechanism of an automobile, described in detail while allowing a maximum view of the car's exterior appearance.

FIGURE 4. A basement shelter whose wall structure and interior area are revealed and emphasized by a cutaway.

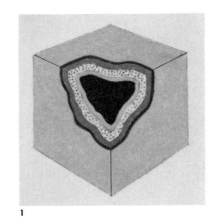

1

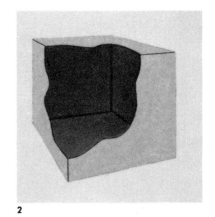

2

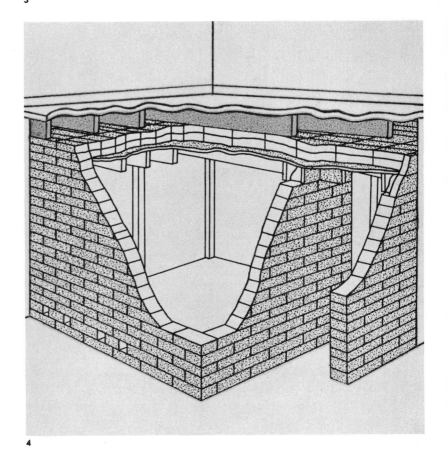

3

4

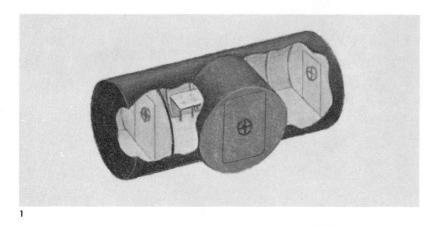

1

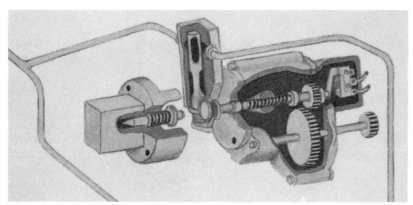

2

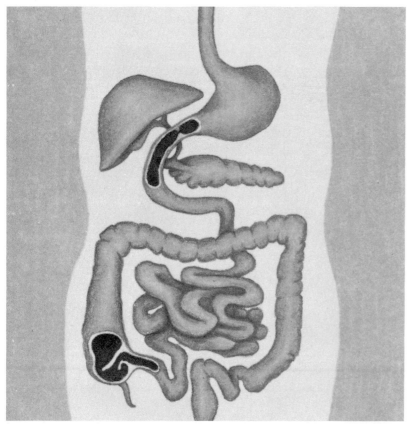

3

REVEALED structure (continued).

FIGURE 1. A compartmental structure whose interior form is emphasized by using a lighter shade in contrast to the darker exterior.

FIGURE 2. Internal mechanical parts revealed by a cutaway, and clarified as light form against a dark interior.

FIGURE 3. The human digestive tract, in which inner intestinal structure is revealed at two places. Here, the surrounding body form is also indicated, but appropriately formalized and subordinated.

REVEALED structure (continued).

FIGURE 1. A cutaway in which the structure of both the enclosing wall and the internal substance are evident. Only the wall portion was removed, showing the internal substance in an otherwise natural condition and emphasizing it with textural description.

FIGURE 2. An engine in which certain internal aspects of its structure are revealed with multiple cutaways. The internal forms are distinguished from the external by darker shading.

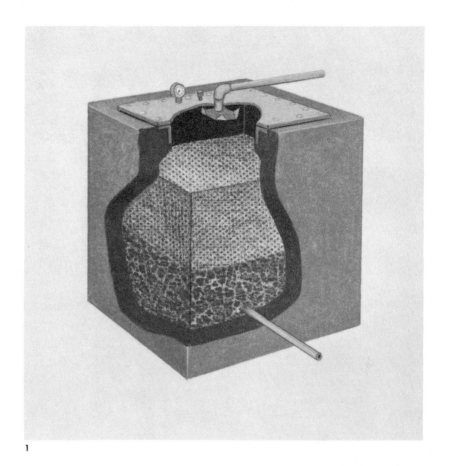

1

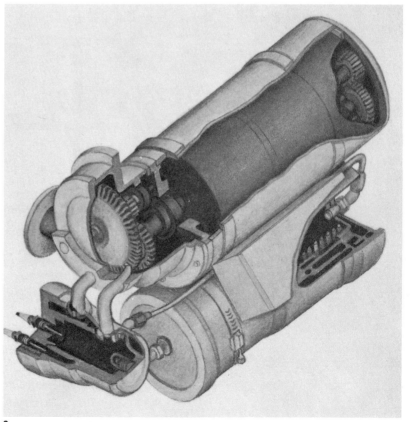

2

1

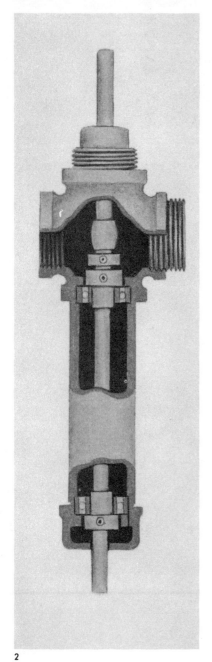

2

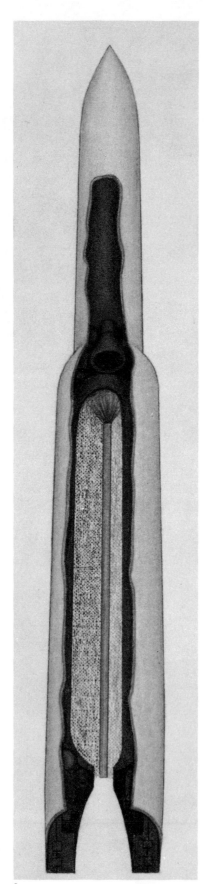

3

REVEALED structure (continued).

FIGURE 1. The interior of a drain pipe emphasized as white to permit sharp description of the valve detail within.

FIGURE 2. A valve mechanism whose containing form is represented to the minimum degree necessary to maintain its identity. This permits a maximum view of the interior.

FIGURE 3. The internal structure of a rocket revealed by a double cutaway which shows the interior of the fuel tank as well as the interior of the rocket as a whole. Here, dark and light values alternate in representing the revealed inner structures.

SEMI-SECTION structure is that which is shown by making two or more imaginary intersecting cuts in the form of the subject. Removal of the resulting segment exposes an area of inner structural substance. Generally, the cuts are conceived as straight and, therefore, produce interior planes of structure.

FIGURE 1. A triple-cut semi-section of a simple cube, showing textural structure.

FIGURE 2. A reversed semi-section which shows the corner foundation of a building.

FIGURE 3. A double-cut semi-section which reveals but does not extend into an internal form.

FIGURE 4. A partial interior view of a regulator, shown by a quadruple-cut that excludes the threaded element in the center.

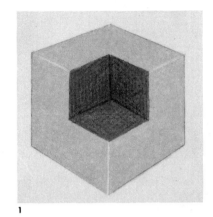

1

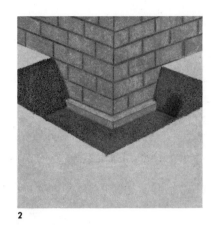

2

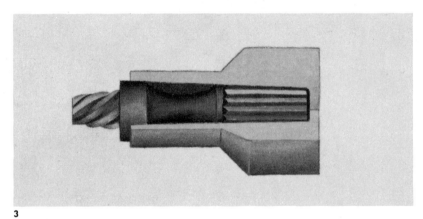

3

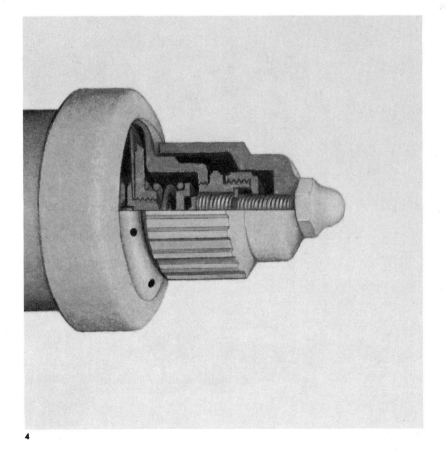

4

1

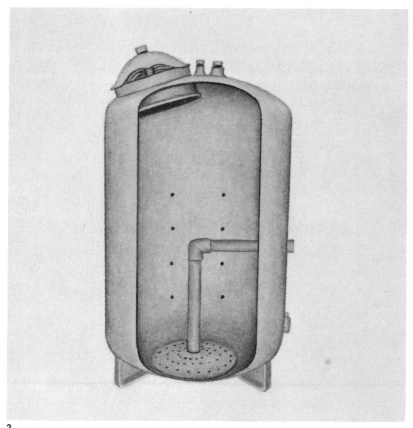

2

SEMI-SECTION structure (continued).

FIGURE 1. The front interior of a jet aircraft shown by a double-cut into the enclosing shell which permits a description of elements within.

FIGURE 2. A semi-section produced with a single cut into the shell of a closed cylindrical object.

SEMI-SECTION structure (continued).

FIGURE 1. An engine interior. Since the cut includes only the central form, it is considered a semi-section even though it reveals only one plane of inner structure. Lighter shading subordinates and differentiates the exterior elements.

FIGURE 2. A double-cut view of an enlarged spark plug base in which lighter shade identifies the planes of the semi-section.

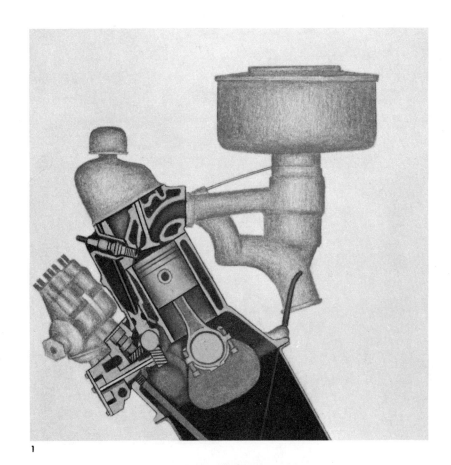

1

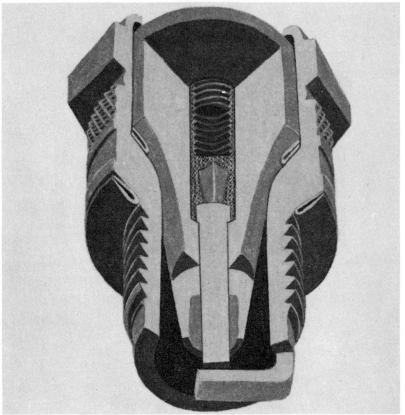

2

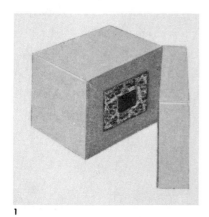

1

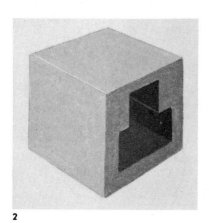

2

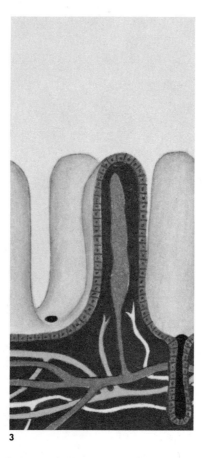

3

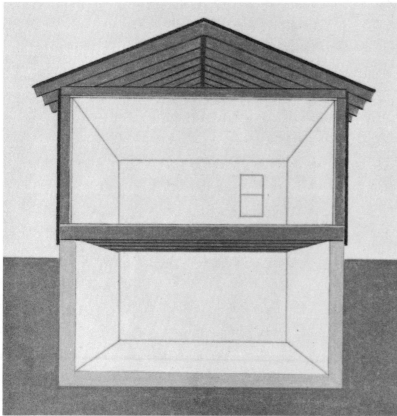

4

SECTION structure is that which is shown by a single, imaginary straight cut through the subject, exposing an entire plane of inner structure. The location of the cut is conceived to afford the best possible view of the subject's internal constitution.

FIGURE 1. A section cut of a cube object, showing its structural core as well as the removed portion.

FIGURE 2. The shaped interior of another cube object, in which the plane of the cut is indicated by a darker shade.

FIGURE 3. An enlarged sectional view of intestinal wall structure, using a dark ground on the inside to permit form description with lighter shades.

FIGURE 4. A section view of a house, including basement and ground elements as well as the upper structure.

SECTION structure (continued).

FIGURE 1. A section view of a mechanical part, showing a connecting bolt not sectioned, so that it can be described in detail for clarity and emphasis.

FIGURE 2. An engine whose sectioned interior is represented in gray, while forms beyond the section plane are shown in black.

FIGURE 3. A center section of a regulator showing (as white) the open areas of its interior through which gas passes. Closed interior spaces are represented as black. Nut and thread elements and portions of springs remain unsectioned for clarity.

FIGURE 4. A piston structure shown through a sectional view. The subject is tilted away from the picture plane to permit an indication of its external form.

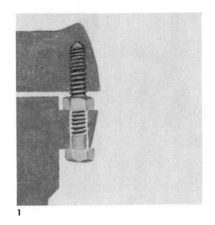

1

2

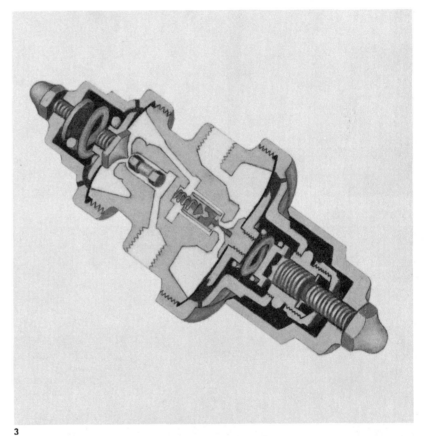

3

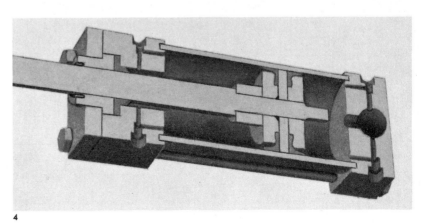

4

89

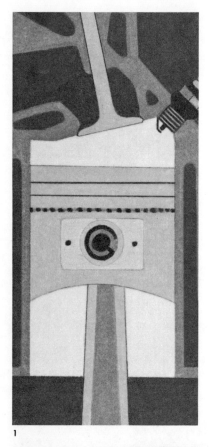

1

2

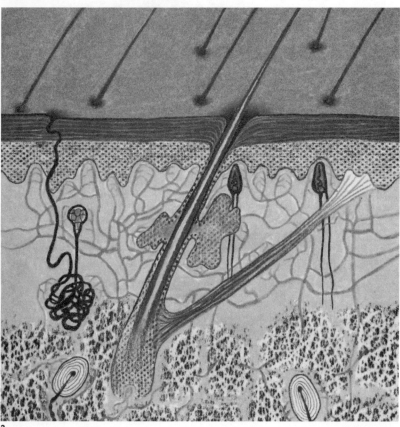

3

SECTION structure (continued).

FIGURE 1. A formalized section view of a piston and its cylinder whose interior is emphasized as white against the darker surroundings.

FIGURE 2. The internal structure of a gladiolus bulb shown by a sectional cut through its center which includes the surrounding earth.

FIGURE 3. An enlarged sectional view of human skin showing its structural elements in detail. Included are hair follicles and a limited view of the external skin surface. The visual description is formalized for clarity.

MULTI-SECTION structure is shown by two imaginary plane cuts through the subject's form, which are at right angles to one another. Therefore, each plane represents an independent section (or cross section) of the subject's structural substance; and, together, they present complimentary views which can convey a sense of the subject's total inner structure.

FIGURE 1. A simple rectangular object with a middle space defined by the black areas. Guidelines serve to relate the two views.

FIGURE 2. An object similar to the preceding one, but showing a different inner space. Here, guidelines indicate the exact location of each section cut.

FIGURE 3. The compound eyes of a fly showing several in a vertical section view and one in a cross section. The structure is visually formalized for clarity.

FIGURE 4. A tank shown as a section on the ground level and as a cross section below, as part of a network of tanks.

FIGURE 5. Section and cross section views of related tools, showing threaded structure as well as gray plane cuts and black interior spaces.

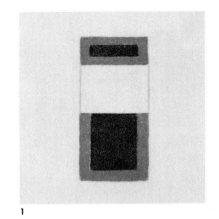

1

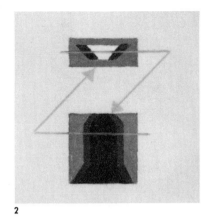

2

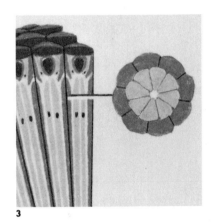

3

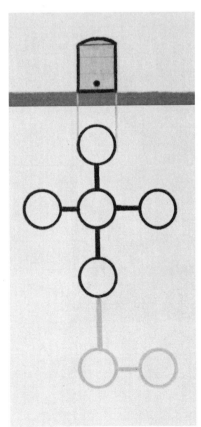

4

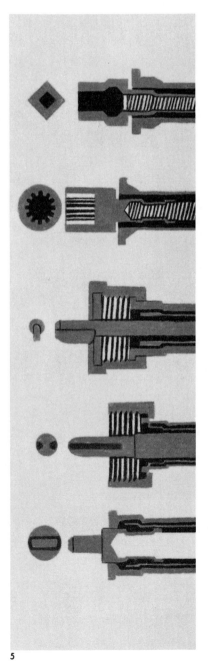

5

91

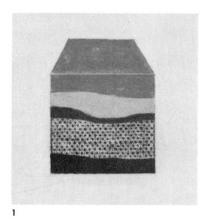
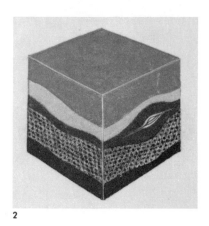

1

2

3

SEGMENT structure, shown by the imaginary removal and representation of the subject substance, is produced by a series of intersecting section cuts similar to those in a semi-section. The planes of the resulting segment display its structure. This type of view is useful for showing the structure of expansive subjects, such as earth, or for subjects whose overall form is irrelevant to the intended idea.

FIGURE 1. A simple cube segment using parallel perspective to emphasize the frontal view of structural layers.

FIGURE 2. A similar segment using angular perspective to reveal differences between two of the sides.

FIGURE 3. A biological segment showing the relationship of surface form (top plane) to inner structure.

FIGURE 4. A geological segment in which the top surface and side section act jointly to show the structure of the cavity.

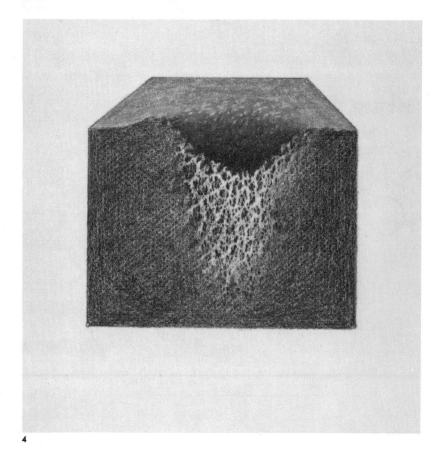

4

92

SEPARATED structure is shown by the imaginary dismembering of the subject's physical parts in a way that reveals their structural role in the formation of the subject. Views of this type can often demonstrate the subject's manner of assembly, as well as its natural structure.

FIGURE 1. A simple cube whose planes are separated on the front side to show the way in which it is formed.

FIGURE 2. A part of the intestines separated to show parasites.

FIGURE 3. A raft showing natural structure and manner of assembly in terms of physical reality.

FIGURE 4. A chair whose components have been separated in part or in whole to show the nature of its construction.

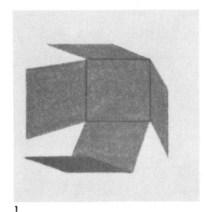

1

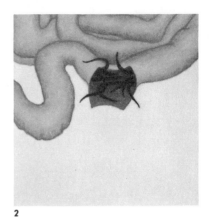

2

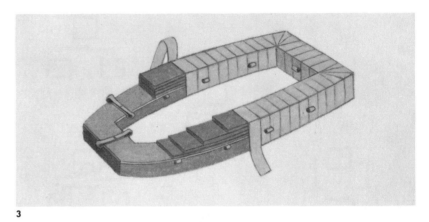

3

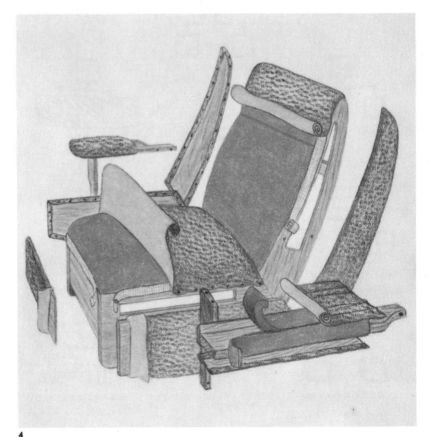

4

93

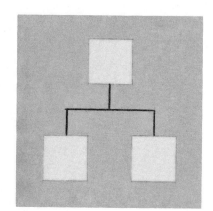

ORGANIZATION

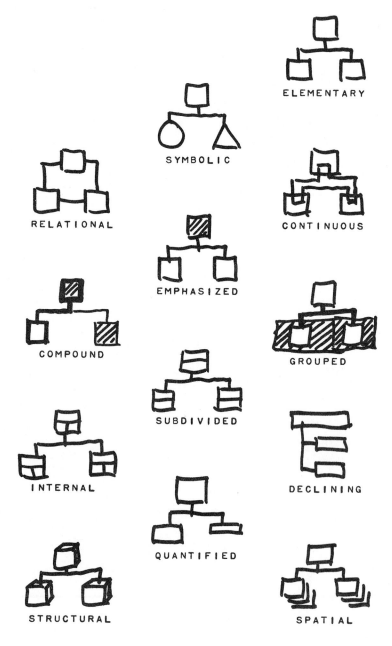

ELEMENTARY

SYMBOLIC

RELATIONAL

CONTINUOUS

COMPOUND

EMPHASIZED

GROUPED

INTERNAL

SUBDIVIDED

DECLINING

STRUCTURAL

QUANTIFIED

SPATIAL

Organization concerns the logical interrelation of elements of a subject in terms of the whole. In the graphic figure, organization logic is generally represented within an abstract context. It can be *elementary* in nature, or more complex in terms of meaning and arrangement. Its form character can be *symbolic* to clarify element meanings, while various *relational* patterns can be used to describe the organization logic. Organization can be shown as *continuous* or specific elements within it can be *emphasized.* Two or more patterns can be integrated into a *compound* organization. Subject elements can be *grouped* or *subdivided* into dual meanings, or shown in terms of their *internal* components. The organization pattern can be *declining* in its arrangement, or *quantified* in its meaning. It can show the *structural* organization of a physical subject, or the *spatial* organization of a subject whose meaning requires a three dimensional arrangement. The following figure models represent design solutions to specific problems in these areas.

ELEMENTARY organization is that in which simple subject elements are given abstract form containers (for words) and are linked into an arrangement which shows their pattern of interrelationship. Generally, rectangular shapes serve well as abstract elements, since they easily maintain a neutral visual identity and are efficient containers for blocks of word forms. Simple linear connectors operate most effectively as a horizontal/vertical framework which utilizes the horizontal and vertical spaces created by the element boxes.

FIGURE 1. A simple organization of subject elements into second and third levels of meaning, using gray shade and black line vocabulary for differentiation (see page 37).

FIGURE 2. A shade value reverse of figure 1, to permit a maximum (black and white) differentiation between boxes and lines.

FIGURE 3. Elongation of the major subject box, for emphasis and/or word space.

FIGURE 4. A subject, its auxiliary member, and four elements.

FIGURE 5. An organization of primary and secondary patterns, in which the secondary pattern builds out of a second-level element. The boxes are elongated for word space.

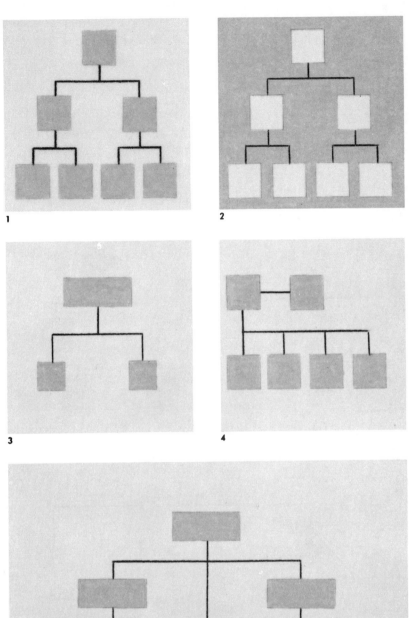

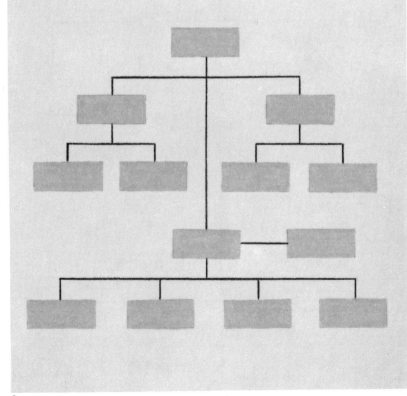

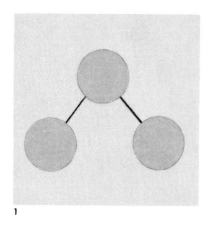

1

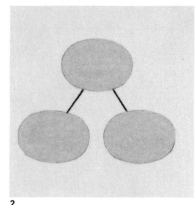

2

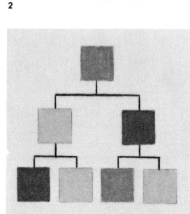

3

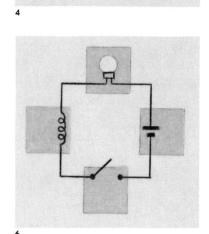

4

5

6

7

8

SYMBOLIC organization shows subject elements whose visual forms express associative or conventional meanings. In the case of the conventional (non-descriptive) symbol, its meaning can be either universally understood or simply assigned (by text or figure key) for temporary use (see also page 106). Visual unity and clarity are primary considerations in creating an effective symbol.

FIGURE 1. A simple pattern using circle forms which act as assigned symbols and permit irregular, diagonal organization.

FIGURE 2. The organization of figure 1 with elliptical element symbols to accommodate word forms more effectively.

FIGURE 3. Different shape structures as assigned symbolic elements.

FIGURE 4. The use of gray shade values to differentiate the symbolic meanings of elements.

FIGURE 5. Assigned symbols which relate in different ways to the parent symbol.

FIGURE 6. Conventionalized electronic symbols with neutral word boxes.

FIGURE 7. Symbolic meaning through subject matter association.

FIGURE 8. Symbolic organization through subject associations.

RELATIONAL organization is that in which the character and arrangement of the connectors act as the decisive factors in showing the nature of the organization. Here, the manner of relationship is most important, and the element boxes perform a dependent role.

FIGURE 1. Diagonal connectors for emphasizing direct relationship.

FIGURE 2. A centralized relationship rather than a declining one.

FIGURE 3. A declining pattern of relationships that are informally suggested rather than explicitly defined.

FIGURE 4. A circuit organization showing parallel relationships.

FIGURE 5. Association of elements and connectors for emphasizing the basic relationship.

FIGURE 6. Relationship of subordinate elements to the parent element, both directly and through intermediate elements.

FIGURE 7. A pattern in which the relationship form is dominant.

FIGURE 8. A pattern in which the elements are formed by the relationship itself.

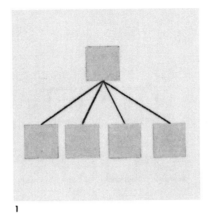

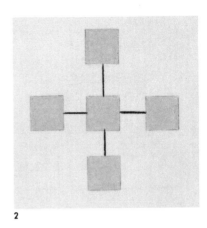

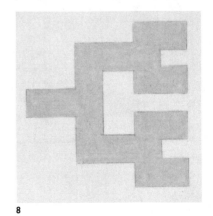

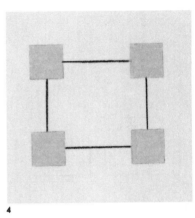

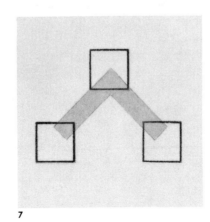

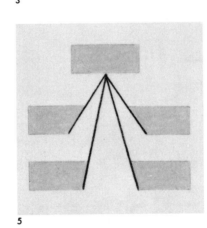

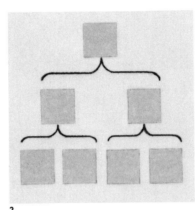

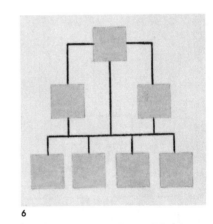

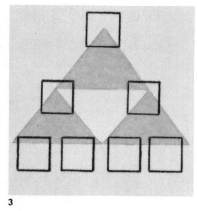

1

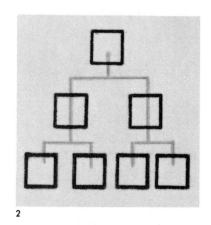

2

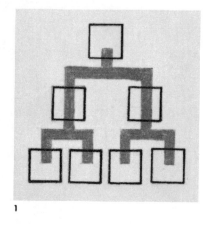

3

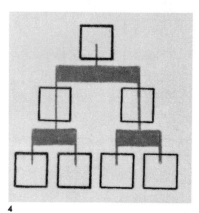

4

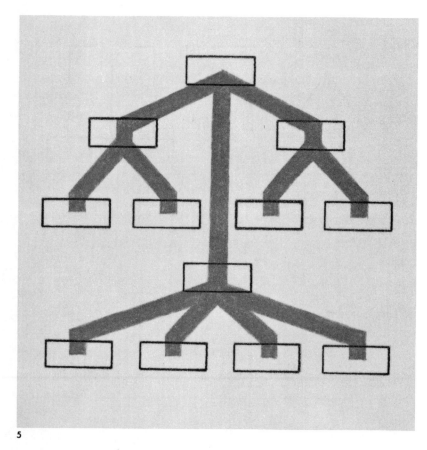

5

CONTINUOUS organization here shows a pattern of related subject elements whose line of interconnection remains direct and unbroken as it passes through intermediate levels. In this case, the relationship itself becomes the primary statement, and subject elements are treated as supporting members.

FIGURE 1. A continuous organization in which the connecting form is the dominant element.

FIGURE 2. A continuous organization in which supporting elements are emphasized and the primary connecting form is subordinated.

FIGURE 3. The primary connecting structure is shown as a pattern of specific (triangular) relationship elements.

FIGURE 4. The relationship structure is shown as a system of elements which parallels (with box forms) the supporting subject elements.

FIGURE 5. A continuous organization structure whose pattern of relationship is emphasized by direct, diagonal inter-connection. Here, the spatial independence of the connecting structure from the boxes eliminates the awkwardness and perspective suggestions usually found in the diagonal connection of rectangular boxes.

EMPHASIZED organization elements show importance in terms of subject meaning. Conversely, visually subordinated elements can indicate meanings of a secondary or auxiliary nature. Visual emphasis and subordination can be created through color value, form structure, relative size, and manner of connection.

FIGURE 1. Emphasis of a third-level element through a darker gray.

FIGURE 2. Lesser emphasis of the same element through outline.

FIGURE 3. Increased size of the parent element to emphasize its role.

FIGURE 4. A declining order of emphasis to indicate declining importance of elements.

FIGURE 5. Subordination of an auxiliary element by lighter gray.

FIGURE 6. Outline subordination, to dissociate the element's order of meaning from the other elements.

FIGURE 7. Greatly enlarged parent box for descriptive text and emphasis.

FIGURE 8. Subordination of related auxiliary element by a weakened (dotted line) connector.

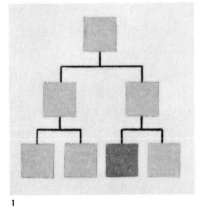
3

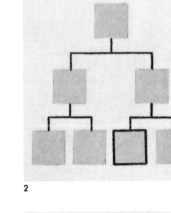

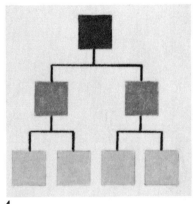
1

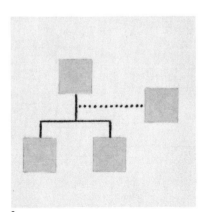
2

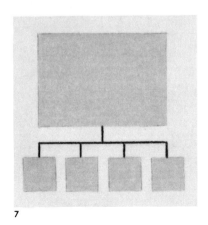
4

5

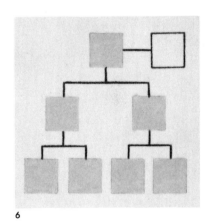
6

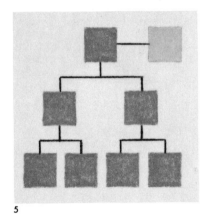
7

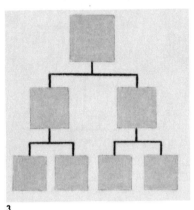
8

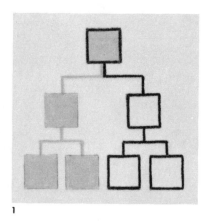

1

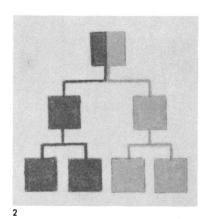

2

COMPOUND organization combines two otherwise independent patterns of related elements into a joint configuration, in which certain elements are shared by both patterns. Differentiation of the form character of the two patterns, in a way that permits joint occupancy of box elements, is essential for showing compound relationships.

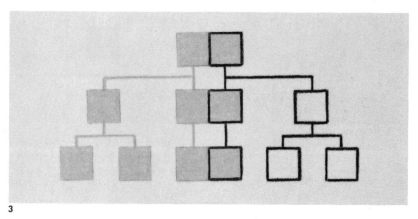

3

FIGURE 1. A compound organization in which elements are differentiated by solid gray and outline form.

FIGURE 2. The same organization using gray shades to emphasize the pattern on the left.

FIGURE 3. Partial sharing of center elements using the form vocabulary of figure 1.

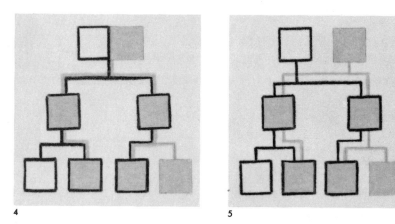

4

5

FIGURE 4. Compound sharing of central subordinate elements and a single but differentiated parent element.

FIGURE 5. Independent parent elements and a compound sharing of central subordinate elements.

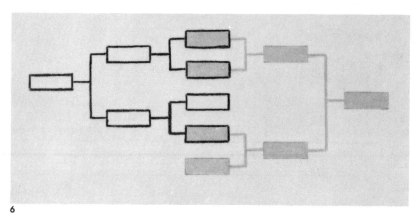

6

FIGURE 6. Compound sharing of third-level elements, organized horizontally for clarity.

GROUPED organization identifies a particular configuration of elements within a larger pattern of relationships, and shows the elements as a related grouping by enclosing them within a unifying form. The unifying form is designed so as not to destroy the sense of the overall organization pattern.

FIGURE 1. A simple grouping of secondary elements using a gray form and reversing the box shades to white.

FIGURE 2. Three progressive groupings representing levels of organization.

FIGURE 3. A grouping similar to figure 1 with an additional secondary grouping which forms a compound and identifies third-level elements.

FIGURE 4. A grouping pattern similar to figure 2, using decreasing gray values to differentiate the groups.

FIGURE 5. A more complex version of the logic of figure 1, in which a third-level element is expanded as a grouping to show its organization.

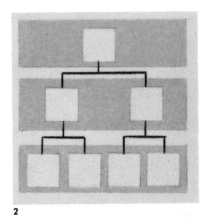

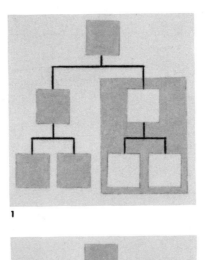

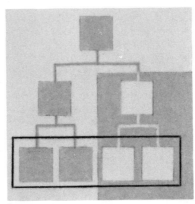

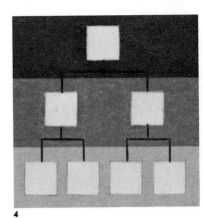

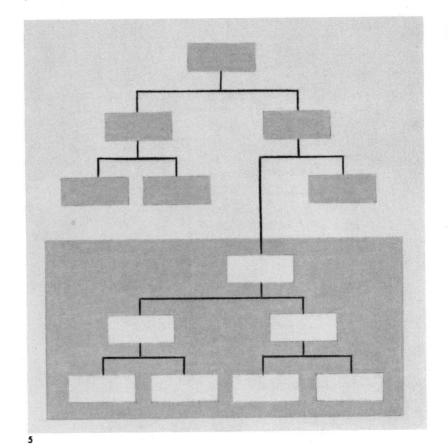

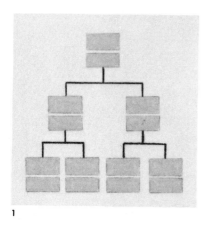

1

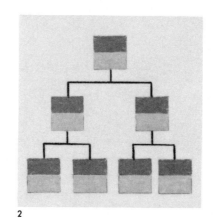

2

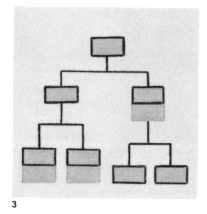

3

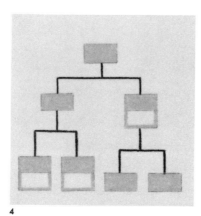

4

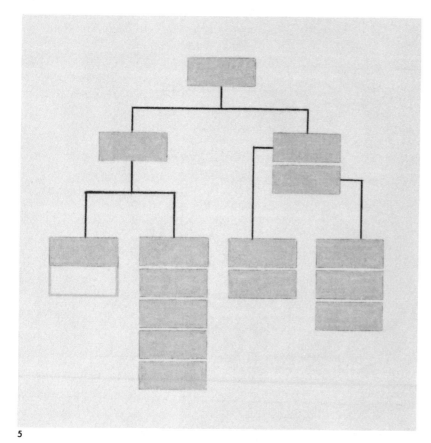

5

SUBDIVIDED organization elements are those which show multiple or complimentary meanings. While being visually differentiated in their internal structure, they act as unified, single elements within the organization pattern.

FIGURE 1. Subdivided elements within a simple organization in which the subdivisions are shown as parallel in importance, and act together as dual meanings.

FIGURE 2. The same pattern in which the lower subdivisions are subordinated with lighter gray to act in a supporting role.

FIGURE 3. Complimentary subdivisions whose gray shapes derive, in meaning, from the primary outlined elements.

FIGURE 4. Complimentary subdivisions which, as gray outlines, relate in a subordinate way to the solid gray primary elements.

FIGURE 5. A complex subdivided organization showing examples of multiple-parallel elements and a subordinate complimentary element.

INTERNAL organization shows the pattern of subordinate parts within an element of a larger organization. In practice, these parts can be represented as a sub-organization, or they can be simply itemized in a consecutive order.

FIGURE 1. Itemized internal parts within a simple organization using negative (white) boxes to show the parts and allowing space at the top of the gray box for the element title.

FIGURE 2. The same organization pattern using a line vocabulary to differentiate the element containers in their sense of meaning.

FIGURE 3. A compound version of figures 1 and 2 in which the secondary gray element as a whole derives specifically from the second internal part of the parent element.

FIGURE 4. A sub-organization of one of the secondary elements of the larger organization.

FIGURE 5. A complex pattern of sub-organizations including a pair of detached element parts which are shown to be organized outside the element itself in terms of their meaning.

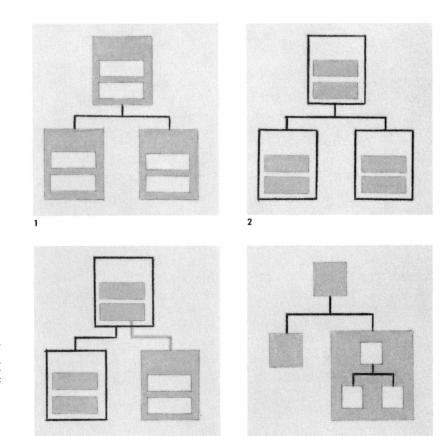

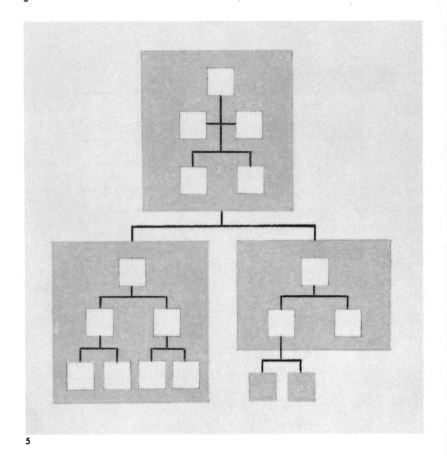

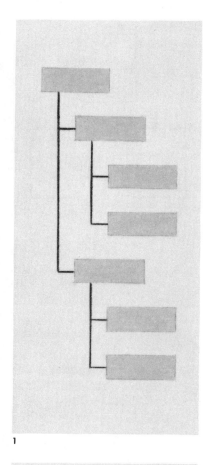

1

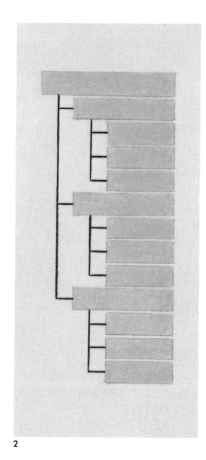

2

DECLINING organization shows the elements of the subject in a downward progression, indicating a sequence in their order as well as a pattern of subordinate relationship. This can be used to relate factors concerning time or procedure to the organizational description. The composition is usually vertical.

FIGURE 1. A simple declining organization showing a succession of element relationships.

FIGURE 2. A compression of declining elements, as in a textual outline, to show the organization as a unified whole.

FIGURE 3. A pattern of declining emphasis showing relative importance through dark and light.

FIGURE 4. A continuous relationship within a declining organization pattern.

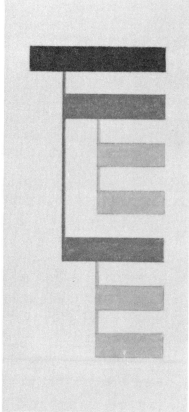

3

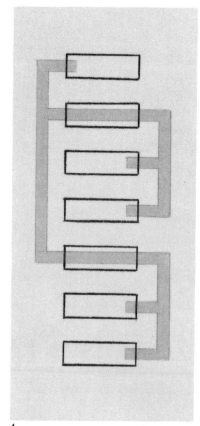

4

QUANTIFIED organization shows the amount of the subject contained by each element in the relationship. These quantities are expressed by the relative sizes of the element boxes. They can be measured in terms of their height, their width, or both, as a composite quantity.

FIGURE 1. A simple quantified organization in which the parent quantity is divided into second and third-level element quantities.

FIGURE 2. A representation of element quantities in terms of two dimensions, to indicate two mutually dependent measurement factors.

FIGURE 3. A measurement of organization amounts in terms of an ordinate scale, to indicate two independent quantitative factors.

FIGURE 4. A phased organization of the subject into subordinate quantity elements.

FIGURE 5. A progressive organization of the parent subject into quantified elements, to relate each successive division to the whole.

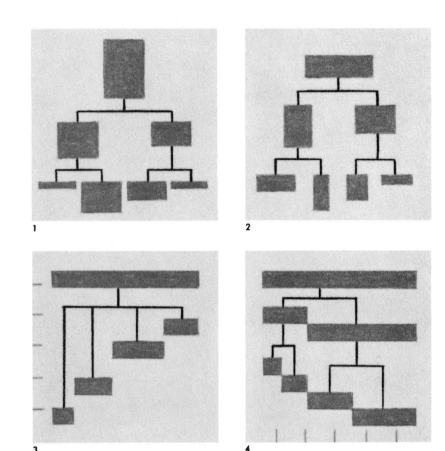

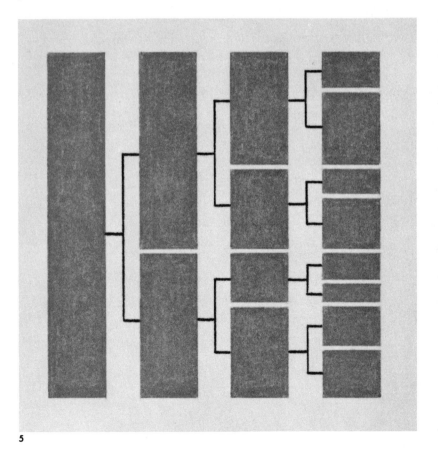

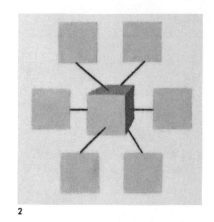

1

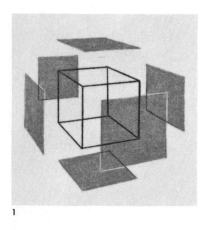

2

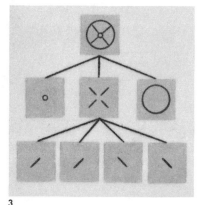

3

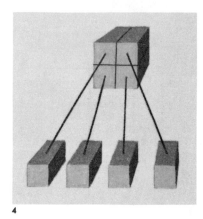

4

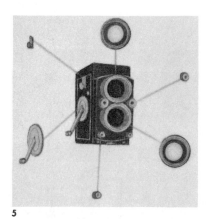

5

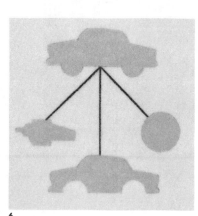

6

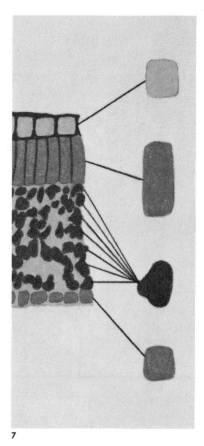

7

STRUCTURAL organization shows the manner in which elements of a physical subject are related to the subject as a whole (see also page 70). Here, the logic of their organization, rather than their compositional appearance, is the primary communicative aim. The context can be objective or symbolic, depending on the problem.

FIGURE 1. The organization of a cube shown in simple perspective outline in which the plane elements are related to the whole.

FIGURE 2. A formalized organization of the cube of figure 1.

FIGURE 3. A symbolic organization of the elements of a wheel.

FIGURE 4. The organization of a cube into component block elements.

FIGURE 5. Selected elements of a camera, shown objectively for clear identification.

FIGURE 6. An automobile, symbolically organized in terms of its parts.

FIGURE 7. The organization of a leaf shown in terms of its internal elements.

SPATIAL organization shows the arrangement of subject elements in depth to permit a third dimension of meaning with respect to their interrelationship. Here, the context can be objective, symbolic, or abstract, depending on the nature of the problem.

FIGURE 1. A simple organization of abstract elements in depth, to show the multiple occurrence of intermediate elements.

FIGURE 2. Another example of the multiple occurrence of intermediate elements in depth, here with symbolic elements individually related to the parent element.

FIGURE 3. A three dimensional organization pattern, utilizing abstract blocks rather than planes to maintain a spatial context. Here, the relationships can vary inwardly as well as vertically and horizontally.

FIGURE 4. The chemical organization of a salt crystal whose physical nature is three dimensional. This figure represents a highly magnified and symbolized view of the crystal's inner pattern of relationship.

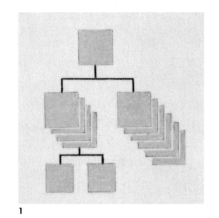

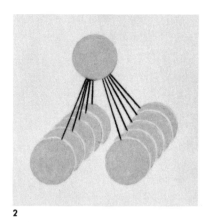

1

2

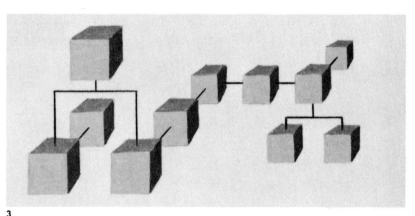

3

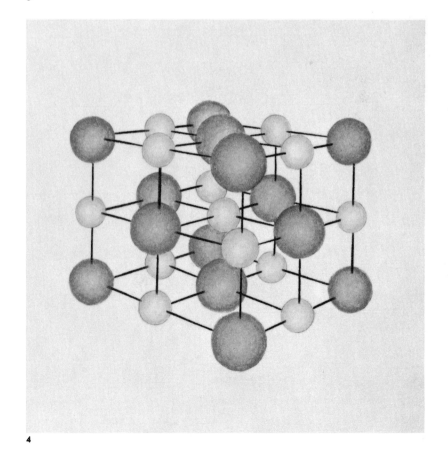

4

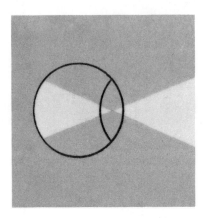

V

TO SHOW *HOW*

How something acts concerns its physical movement, system of flow in relation to component parts, or process as a succession of related events. It is obvious that all three of these aspects, and particularly the last two, are closely related in meaning. Movement can mean a physical process; system can mean abstract movement; process can mean procedural system. However, these aspects also have their differences. Each indicates a different attitude toward the nature of motion, and presents a different view in showing *how* something acts. It is important to separate these aspects, since each permits the communication of specific ideas that otherwise could not be shown clearly. Here, movement, system, and process will be considered independently, and explored as primary problem areas.

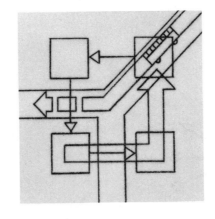

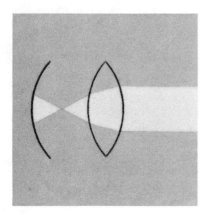

1
MOVEMENT

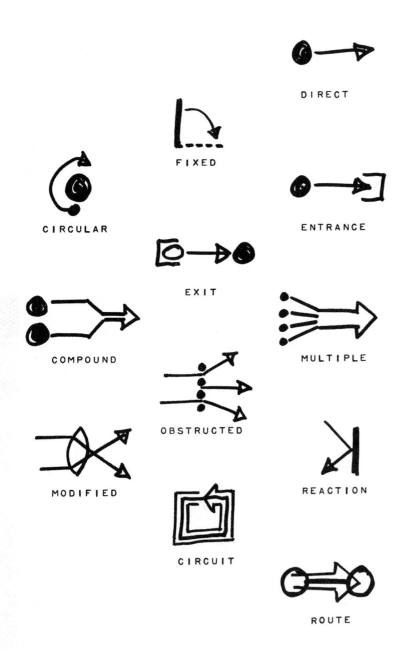

DIRECT

FIXED

CIRCULAR

ENTRANCE

EXIT

COMPOUND

MULTIPLE

OBSTRUCTED

MODIFIED

REACTION

CIRCUIT

ROUTE

Movement concerns the physical action or behavior pattern of a subject in motion. In the graphic figure, the arrow form acts as a conventional symbol to convey the idea of movement. Therefore, the movement figure is usually symbolic in its general terms of meaning. Using the arrow symbol, a subject element can show *direct* movement, *fixed* movement, such as a changing position, or *circular* movement. The movement can indicate the *entrance* or *exit* of the element. Subject elements can be joined in a *compound* movement, or grouped (or massed) in a *multiple* motion. A moving substance can be *obstructed* and changed in its course, or *modified* in its behavior as a result of passing through an interfering element. The subject can also be shown in a *reaction* movement, as a result of previous action, in terms of a continuous *circuit,* or as a movement *route* between stations. The following figure models represent design solutions to specific problems in these areas.

110

DIRECT movement of a subject element can be shown by visually associating it, as a symbol, with an arrow form whose path and head indicate its direction. In general, the arrow form is represented in lighter form than that of the subject, to indicate its intangible nature.

FIGURE 1. The intended movement of four different subjects, each with an arrow form appropriate to its own form.

FIGURE 2. Four kinds of intended movement expressing ideas of slowness, velocity, probability, and irregularity.

FIGURE 3. Four kinds of patterns expressing intended and completed motion, showing both origins and destinations.

FIGURE 4. Subjects in motion, both singly and in series; and completed motion, showing past positions and past stages.

FIGURE 5. The movement pattern of a bus terminal showing variations of bus positions and movements: acceleration, deceleration, etc. (see page 38).

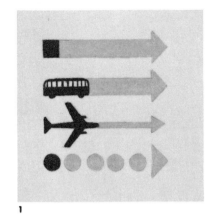
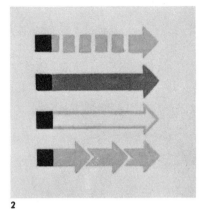

1

2

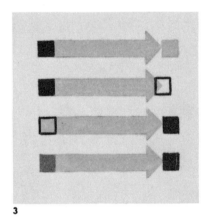
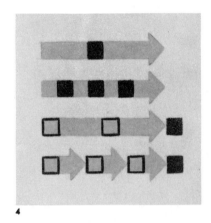

3

4

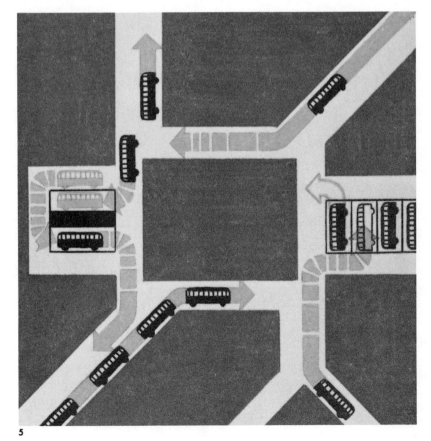

5

111

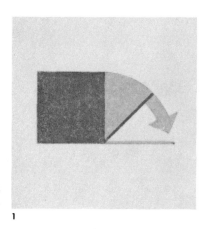

1

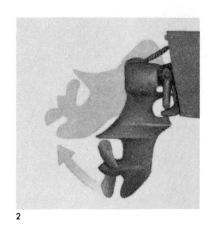

2

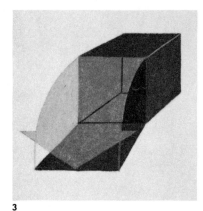

3

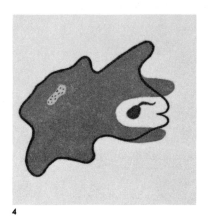

4

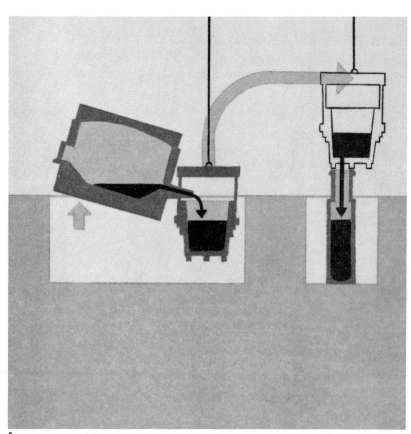

5

FIXED movement shows the motion of a subject element which is partially attached to a fixed position. In this case the movement pattern is modified to produce simply a change of position relative to the place and manner in which the element is fixed.

FIGURE 1. The side of a square object connected to the lower right corner of the square and swinging downward toward a new position.

FIGURE 2. The indicated position change of an outboard motor swinging on an axis attached to a boat.

FIGURE 3. The swinging open of a side of a simple cube connected along the lower edge.

FIGURE 4. An amoeba changing the position of its right side forms to absorb a small organism. Here, the form movement pattern is evident without the use of arrow forms.

FIGURE 5. Tapping and pouring actions in a steel mill, showing a variety of movements relative to fixed positions.

CIRCULAR movement shows an element acting in a circular direction around a center. The circle itself may not be completed, or it may not be a true circle. The center may or may not be embodied by a second object.

FIGURE 1. The compound circular movements of one element around another, and a third (subordinate) element around the first.

FIGURE 2. A pendulum action following but not completing a circular path. Positions of maximum swing are indicated.

FIGURE 3. A pulley action in which both circular and direct movements are indicated.

FIGURE 4. A gear mechanism showing complex circular movement associated with a fixed position.

FIGURE 5. The trajectory and landing pattern of a space vehicle moving in a curved rather than a purely circular path. This figure represents a symbolic description in terms of natural reality that conveys a full visual report of the event.

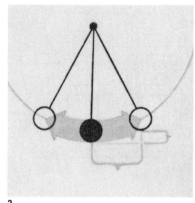

1

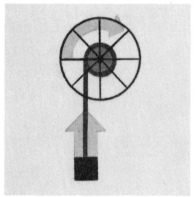

2

3

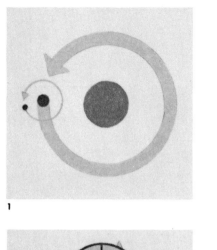

4

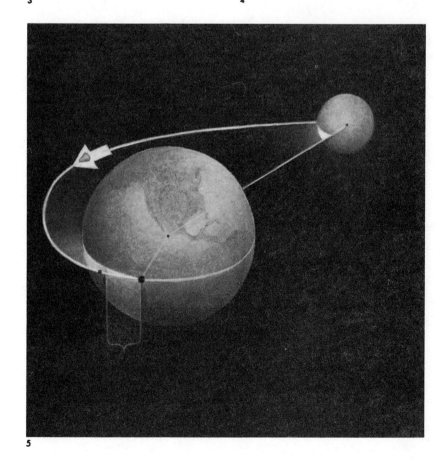

5

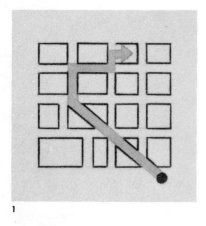

1

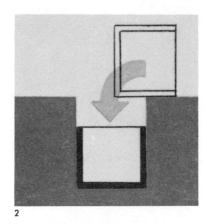

4

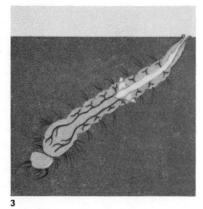

2

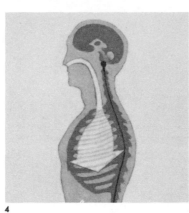

3

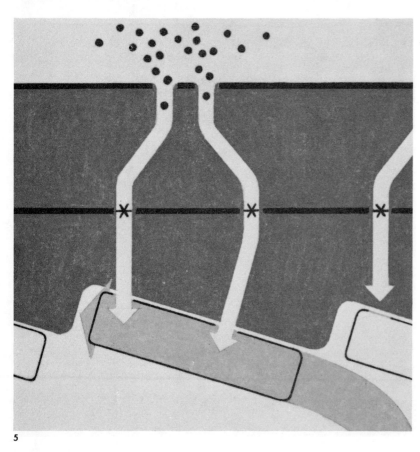

5

ENTRANCE movement shows the action of an element as it approaches and goes into a receiving form. Typically, the receiving form acts as a terminal for the movement pattern of the element, or it modifies the pattern of the moving element.

FIGURE 1. The movement pattern of an element within a network of blocks preliminary to its entrance.

FIGURE 2. The turning motion of a physical form resulting in its entrance into a receiving hole.

FIGURE 3. The entrance of air into a water insect. Motion, in this case, is by a substance rather than an object.

FIGURE 4. The entrance movement of air into human lungs, and its expansion to occupy the lung area.

FIGURE 5. A passenger bus terminal showing the entrance movement of a bus into its loading area, and the generalized entrance patterns of people moving through the terminal and into the bus.

EXIT movement shows the action of an element as it leaves a containing form or structure. The element itself can be either an object or a substance, and can originate from a particular location or from a general source.

FIGURE 1. A spherical object emerging from its indicated place within a cube structure. No arrow symbol is necessary, since the suggestion of movement is obvious.

FIGURE 2. The past motion of an element which moved out of its place of origin and through a network of blocks.

FIGURE 3. A gland secretion pattern, showing fluid substance of various origins moving through and out of the containing channels.

FIGURE 4. The movement of concentrated gas (dark gray) out of its tank and into a regulator, where its pressure is reduced (light gray). The gas then leaves the regulator through an exit tube.

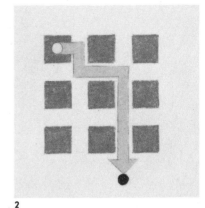

1

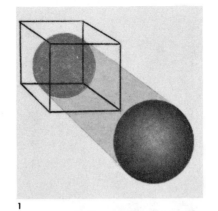

2

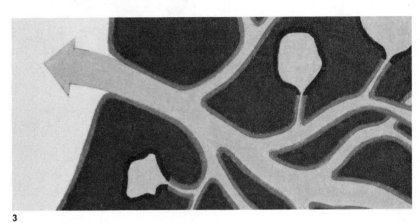

3

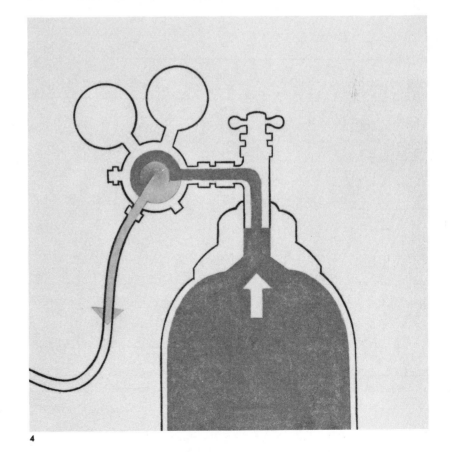

4

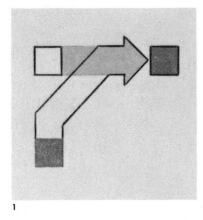

1

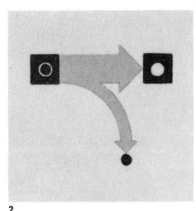

2

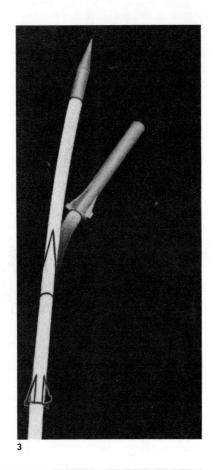

3

COMPOUND movement shows the independent actions of multiple elements which at a given place cooperate in a joint action. The joint movement can be a cause or an effect of the individual movements, and can show the origins or destinations of the elements, or both. Here, visual differentiation of movement patterns is essential.

FIGURE 1. Two different elements joining to form a combined element as well as a combined movement pattern.

FIGURE 2. A single element in motion. From the center, a smaller, secondary element disengages and moves off in a different direction.

FIGURE 3. A rocket in flight, where the primary stage is shown to disconnect and fall off to one side while the secondary stage continues on its course.

FIGURE 4. The symbolized movement of people in and out of a moving chain of rapid transit vehicles.

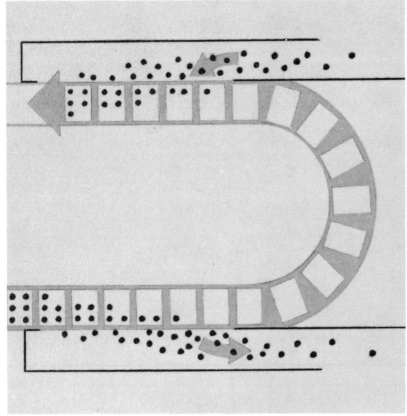

4

MULTIPLE movement shows the combining or combined action of a number of elements within a specific pattern of activity. While the specific elements can be individually represented, they can also be shown to act as a concentrated mass without being specifically differentiated.

FIGURE 1. The collection of individual elements to form a mass movement within a street network.

FIGURE 2. The movement pattern of multiple streams of water passing through the sprinkler head of a hose.

FIGURE 3. The mass movement of air into an engine and its separation into multiple currents within.

FIGURE 4. The multiple movement of impulses toward the cell body of a human motor neuron, showing the interwoven paths of individual impulses as they travel along the association neuron lines.

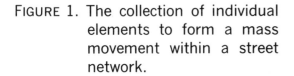

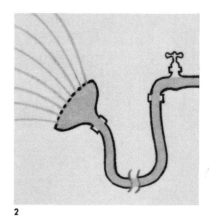

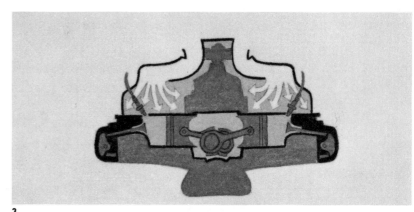

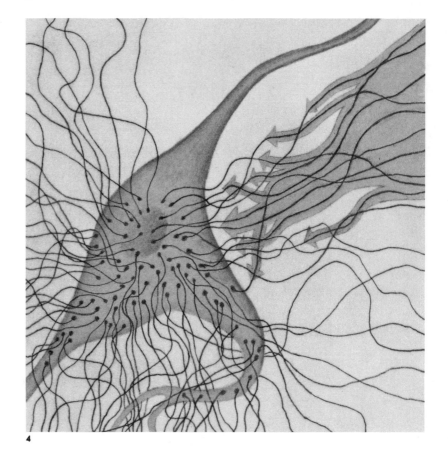

117

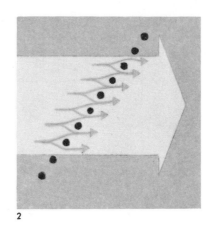

1

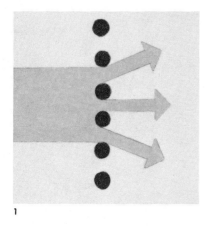

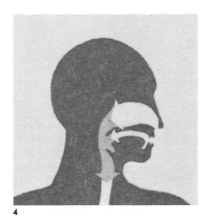

2

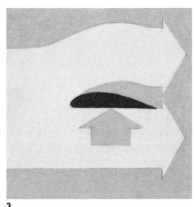

3

4

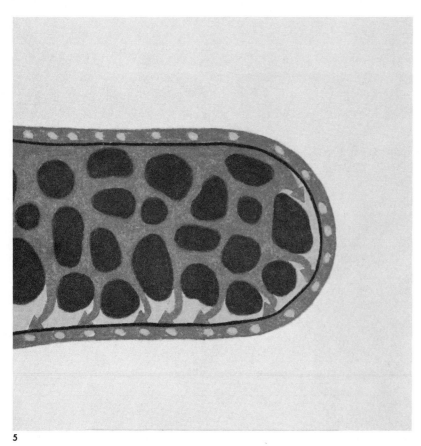

5

OBSTRUCTED movement shows the broken or divided course of a substance as it moves around an interrupting structure. Here, mass movement patterns are shown, rather than individual elements in motion. The movement patterns themselves are treated as fluid, in relation to specific structural features which they encounter.

FIGURE 1. The breakup of a moving substance into three independent directions as a result of colliding with a line of fixed structures.

FIGURE 2. The internal secondary motions produced by the primary movement of a substance through a line of structural elements.

FIGURE 3. The division of an air flow into two individual currents as it encounters a wing form. An upward lift on the wing is also indicated, as a resultant effect.

FIGURE 4. The movement of air into the human body, obstructed by the natural features of nasal and oral passages.

FIGURE 5. The obstructed movement of human blood (middle gray) as it passes around tissue cells (dark gray). Here, the fragmented movements return to the common current from which they originated.

MODIFIED movement shows the behavior of a substance as it passes through an interfering element. This means that the substance and the element must be constituted to enable such internal passage and be represented in visual form which conveys that impression.

FIGURE 1. The refraction of light rays passing through a convex lens, modifying their paths toward a focal intersection.

FIGURE 2. The refraction of a beam of light as it passes through the concave surfaces of a lens, which diffuses the light.

FIGURE 3. The behavior of light as an image carrier in a camera whose lens focuses the light (as in figure 1) and reverses the image.

FIGURE 4. The refraction of light as it passes through water, modifying its direction from what it would normally have been.

FIGURE 5. A spectroscopic refraction of light modifying its normal character to reveal the color spectrum of which it is composed. This figure could be improved by the use of actual color hues, rather than the shades of gray represented here.

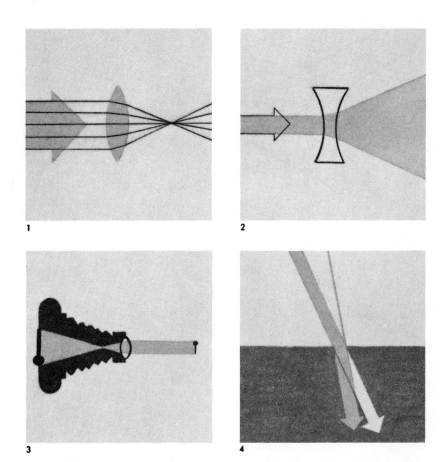

119

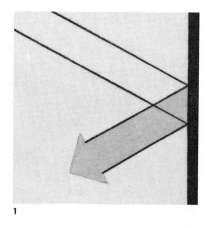

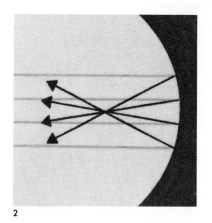

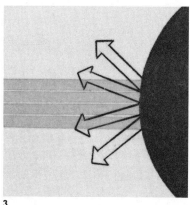

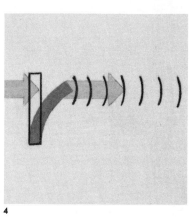

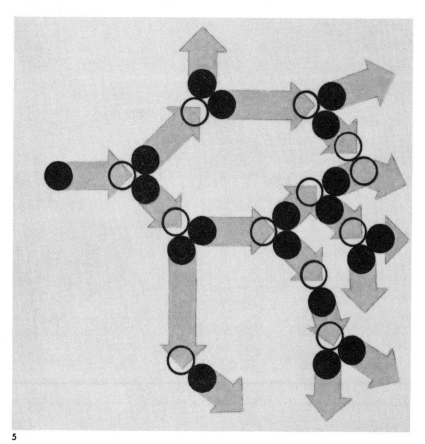

REACTION movement shows the cause and effect relationship produced by the collision of one element or substance into another. The resulting behavior pattern is of primary importance, and it should receive visual emphasis.

FIGURE 1. The behavior pattern of light as it bounces off a flat surface, as a reflection.

FIGURE 2. The behavior of individual light rays as they reflect from a concave surface.

FIGURE 3. The behavior of light beams as they reflect from a convex surface.

FIGURE 4. Wave motion produced by the impact of a force directed against a physical element.

FIGURE 5. A chain reaction pattern produced by the initial action of one element colliding into two others.

CIRCUIT movement shows the course taken by an element or substance as it passes through a specific structure and returns to its point of origin. The implication is that the substance is in a continuous pattern of circulation. In some cases only a part of the total circuit pattern must be shown, since its movement path, rather than its completion, is the important factor to be shown.

FIGURE 1. A simple circuit pattern showing movement within a road network.

FIGURE 2. A simple electronic circuit showing the movement of electricity over a wiring system to which a light bulb is attached.

FIGURE 3. A portion of a more complex electronic circuit showing the passage of electricity. Here, a variety of conventional (electronic) symbols are used.

FIGURE 4. A human capillary bed showing the movement of blood between arterioles (dark) and venules (light) as a part of its total circuit movement.

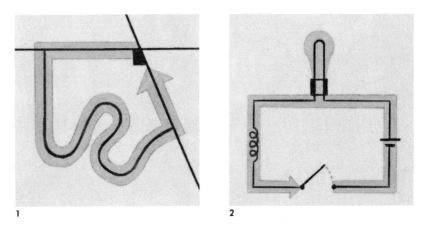

1

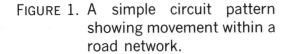

2

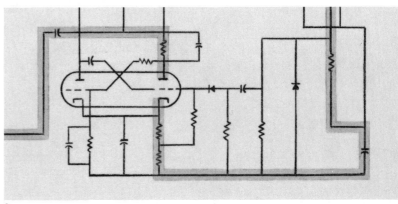

3

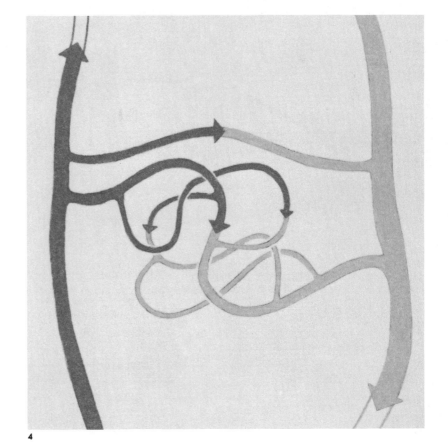

4

121

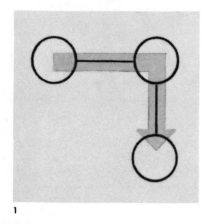

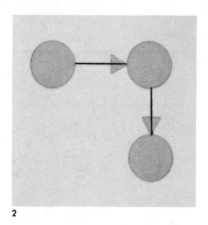

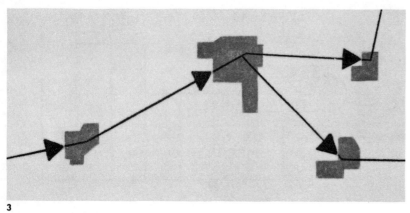

1

2

3

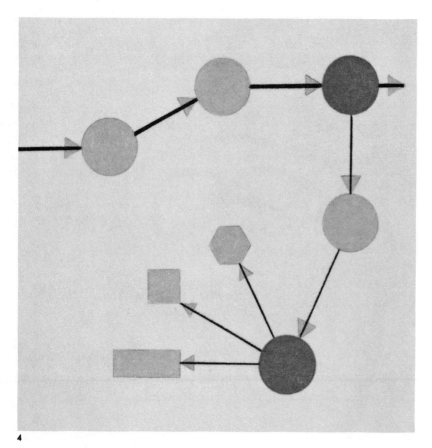

4

ROUTE movement shows the motion or intended motion of an element along a course of fixed structure in which the motion begins at a point of origin and ends at a terminal point. The indication of direction rather than a description of the path (provided by the structure) is frequently sufficient to convey the idea.

FIGURE 1. A simple route indicating movement through an intermediate element between the origin and the terminal element.

FIGURE 2. The same route in which the fixed station elements are more fully characterized and the movement is simply indicated by directional arrowheads associated with the route links.

FIGURE 3. A transportation route showing town areas as station elements and directional arrowheads integrated with the route link forms.

FIGURE 4. A complex transportation route employing the logic of figure 2 to show primary and secondary route links as well as differentiated station elements.

ROUTE movement (continued).

FIGURE 1. A double transportation route with opposite movements showing intersections and passage through an intermediate station.

FIGURE 2. A double transportation route with opposite movements showing multiple reversing loops at a central station intersection, and intermediate station sidings.

FIGURE 3. Three differentiated transportation routes joined as a system at a central station intersection.

FIGURE 4. Three individual transportation routes quantified in width to indicate volume of traffic, and paired closely to permit a visual estimate of the total quantity moving in each direction from the central station (see page 197).

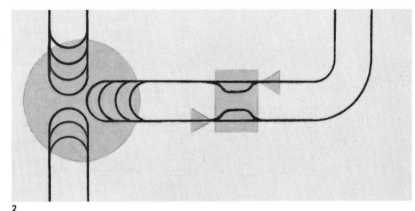

1

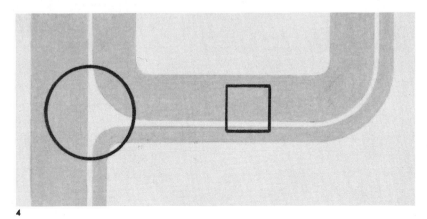

2

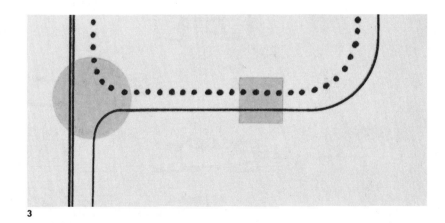

3

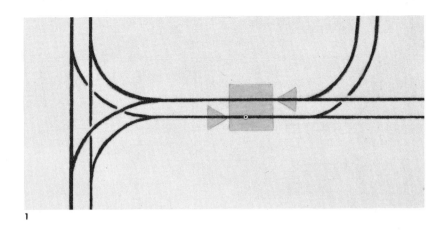

4

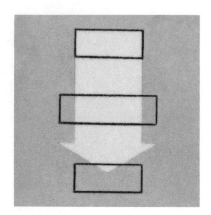

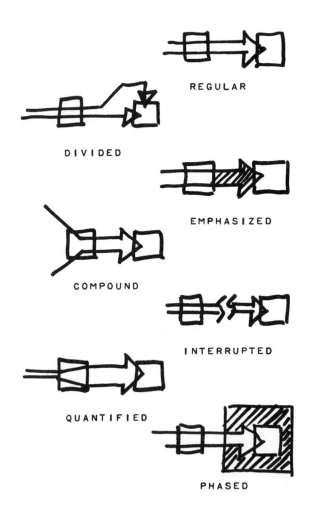

REGULAR

DIVIDED

EMPHASIZED

COMPOUND

INTERRUPTED

QUANTIFIED

PHASED

System concerns the pattern of operation of a subject in terms of its interdependent elements. The logic of an action, rather than its reality, is important here. Therefore, abstract elements as well as symbolic flow forms are employed. In the graphic figure, a *regular* system flow can assume a variety of patterns, depending on the specific problem. The system can also be *divided* to express multiple operations or *emphasized* at one place or another to identify an important segment. Differentiated idea elements can be shown in a *compound* flow arrangement, or the flow can be *interrupted* to reduce or enlarge its detail. Also, the flow can be *quantified* by varying the width of its form or *phased* by differentiating the environmental areas through which it passes. The following figure models represent design solutions to specific problems in these areas.

REGULAR system flow shows a pattern of operation which maintains continuity in its structure and character. It can otherwise move through different routes depending on its functional nature. Often called a "flow" chart, the flow itself and the elements through which it moves constitute the basic forms which make the system.

FIGURE 1. A simple system whose subject flows through four elements arranged in a squared composition for spatial economy and visual unity (see page 39).

FIGURE 2. The same system arranged in a circular pattern to enhance the continuity of flow.

FIGURE 3. A system whose element symbols are arranged in terms of relative subject locations, which results in an eccentric flow pattern.

FIGURE 4. A flow pattern similar to figure 1 in which the four elements are shown as parts of a unified whole.

FIGURE 5. A system whose flow changes character in a regular fashion through a gradual change in shade value. This would indicate an evolving change in the subject itself, which passes through elements of three different identities.

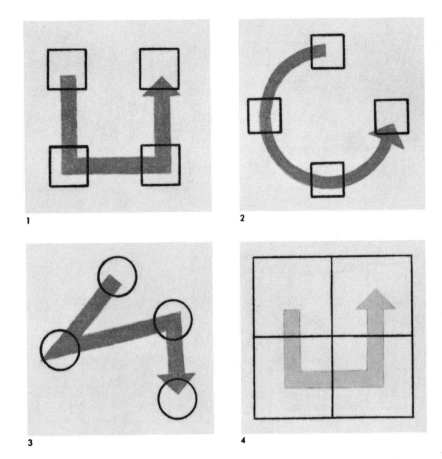

1

2

3

4

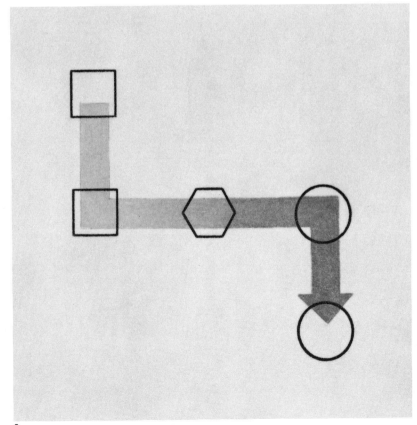

5

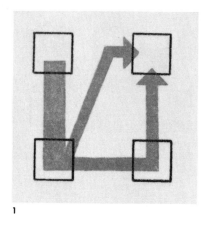

1

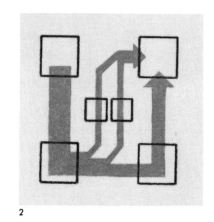

4

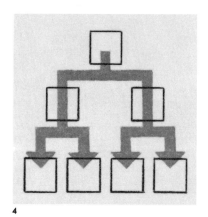

2

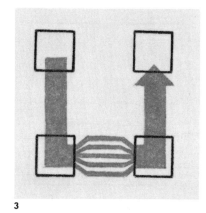

3

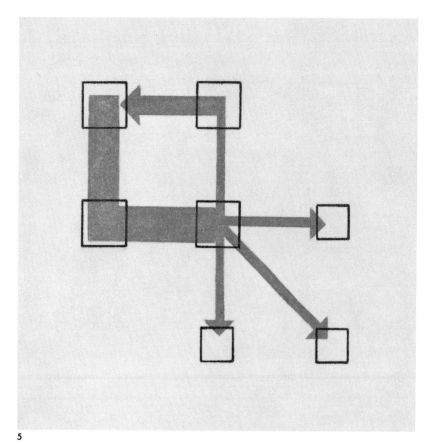

5

DIVIDED system flow shows a pattern which splits into two or more separate or alternative functions. The different flow lines can proceed to independent conclusions, meet at the same conclusion, or reunite and proceed as a combined flow to a single conclusion.

FIGURE 1. A system whose subject flow divides at the second element, creating a bypass route to the conclusion as well as a regular route through the third element.

FIGURE 2. A system showing two subordinate alternatives to the main flow, dividing and passing through minor elements.

FIGURE 3. The division of an intermediate flow segment into individual lines, to show their independent action between the second and third elements.

FIGURE 4. A dividing and subdividing flow creating an expanding system of subject elements.

FIGURE 5. A more complex system division showing three independent concluding flows and one expanding flow return to the originating element.

EMPHASIZED system flow shows dominant and subordinated segments of subject operation, through shade value and structural character. Here, a subordinate pattern can act either as a part of the main flow or as an independent alternative flow.

FIGURE 1. A simple system showing emphasis of the concluding flow segment through darker value.

FIGURE 2. Emphasis of the concluding flow segment by a structural outline, to maintain constant identity in terms of shade value and to associate the flow with the third element subject.

FIGURE 3. A subordinated alternative flow as a modification of the pattern shown in figure 1 on page 126.

FIGURE 4. A diagonal alternative flow to omit the second element, subordinated by a lighter value.

FIGURE 5. A larger system showing a pattern of diminance and subordination. Here, variations in flow structure and value create a complex order of relative emphasis.

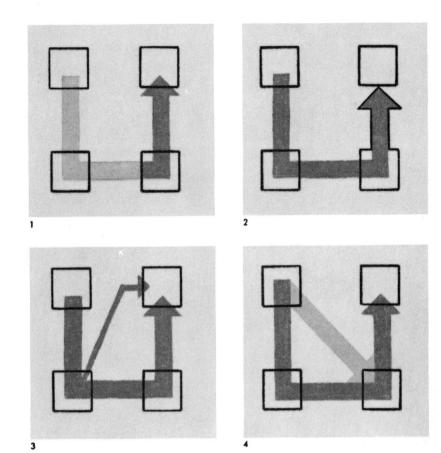

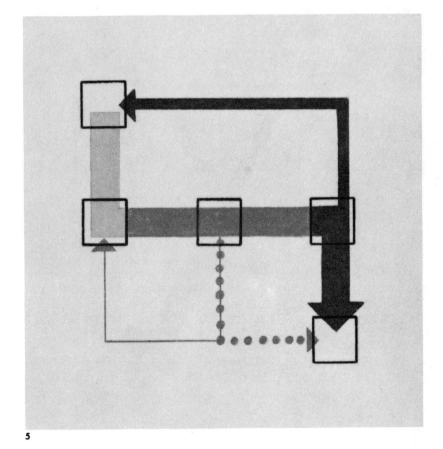

127

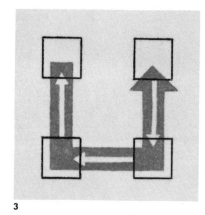

1

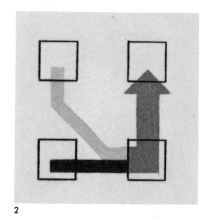

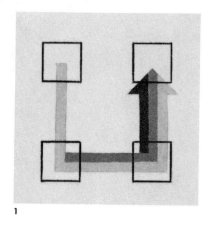

3

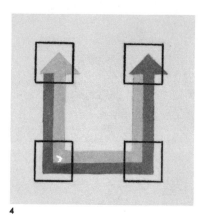

2

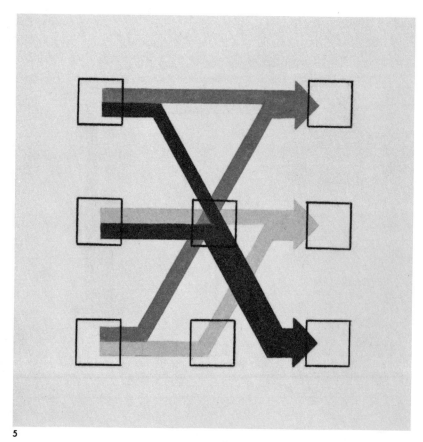

5

COMPOUND system shows the operation of two or more independent subject flows which at some point act jointly to produce a commonly shared pattern. While relative emphasis may be an apparent by-product of varying shade values, in this case, their differentiating function is more important.

FIGURE 1. A compound system in which flow components originate at different elements, and proceed all together toward the concluding element.

FIGURE 2. Two separate flows from two separate originating elements uniting in the third element and proceeding as a whole to the concluding element.

FIGURE 3. A compound system composed of a major flow and a subordinate reverse flow, to indicate subject return.

FIGURE 4. A compound reverse system in which parallel flows move toward the conclusion and return to the originating element.

FIGURE 5. A compound of three flows originating in mixed pairs and moving through a system in which similar segments unite and proceed to individual concluding elements.

INTERRUPTED system is where the flow pattern is broken to omit unnecessary or irrelevant portions, or where enlargement of the flow form is required in order to describe its composition. In such a case, break lines or brackets are used to indicate interruption of the natural continuity of flow.

FIGURE 1. Interruption of a simple flow to eliminate an unnecessary intermediate segment.

FIGURE 2. A shaded separation of elements as well as a flow pattern, to indicate interruption of the entire system.

FIGURE 3. An enlarged intermediate flow segment showing the flow structure in terms of its components.

FIGURE 4. The removal of an irrelevant flow segment indicated below in a smaller scale for secondary reference.

FIGURE 5. The enlargement of a complex flow subject to differentiate its constituent elements, one of which represents the subordinate segment which moves to a minor concluding element.

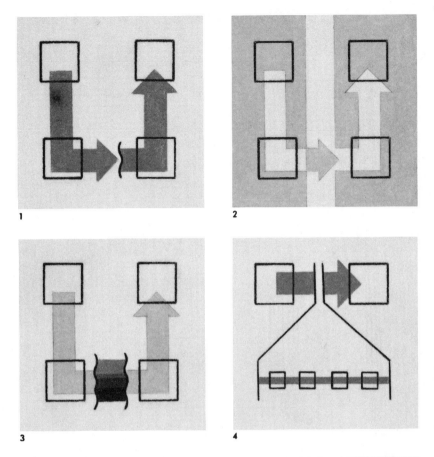

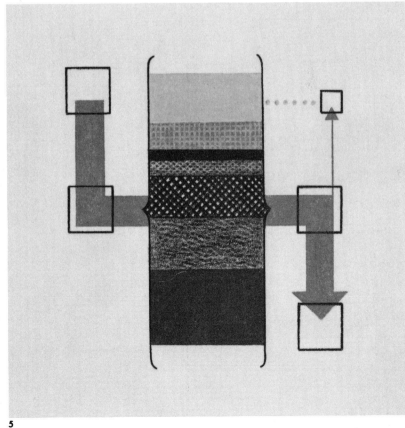

129

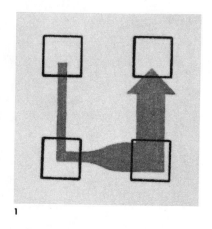

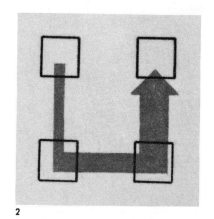

1

2

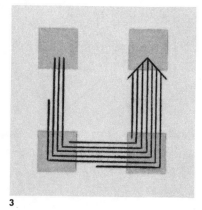

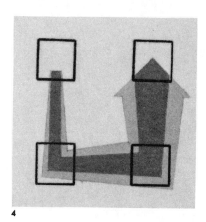

3

4

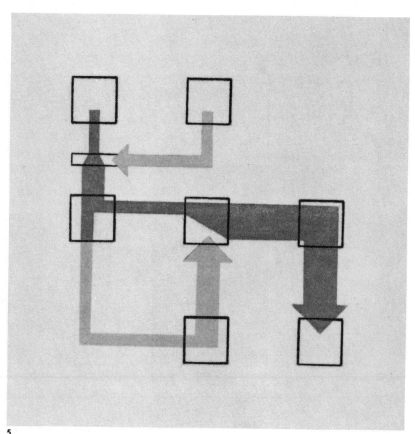

5

QUANTIFIED system shows the relative amount of flow as well as its pattern of operation. Quantitative variation is represented by variations in flow width which can be scaled in direct proportion to actual subject amounts.

FIGURE 1. A simple system showing quantitative increase between the second and third elements.

FIGURE 2. The same system showing increase as a direct product of flow intersection with intermediate elements.

FIGURE 3. Quantitative flow increase represented by scaled linear form structure, to enable visual measurement.

FIGURE 4. Progressive quantitative increase shown in terms of primary and secondary amounts.

FIGURE 5. A complex quantification of system flow where primary (dark) and secondary (light) amounts compliment one another, and where quantitative change is a product of flow intersection with elements.

130

PHASED system flow shows the organization of the subject pattern into operational phases, which can include either the flow line or the network of fixed elements, or both. Any one or all of the system parts may be shown within a phase area.

FIGURE 1. A simple system in which the entire concluding half is shown as a specific phase.

FIGURE 2. A similar system in which the last two elements are enlarged and joined to act together as a unified phase.

FIGURE 3. A system in which the flow pattern is shown as a product of three related phases, which affect but do not include the box elements.

FIGURE 4. A network of phased box elements in which the flow acts as a relating but otherwise independent pattern.

FIGURE 5. Three overlapping phases which organize both the flow pattern and the element boxes into a totally phased system. The concluding phase itself shows a return flow to an intermediate element.

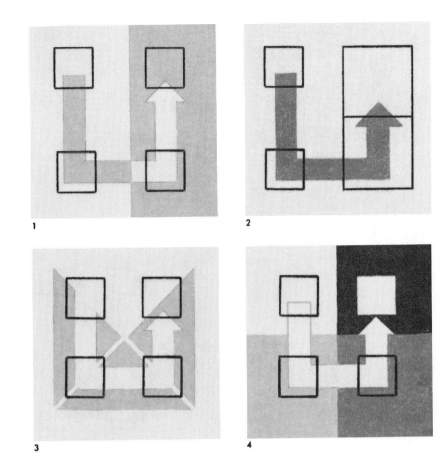

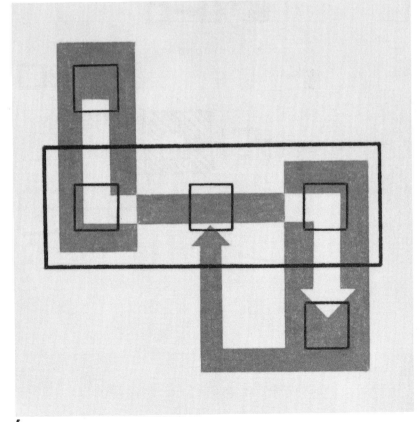

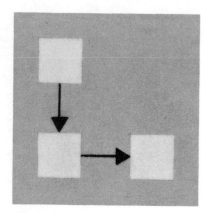

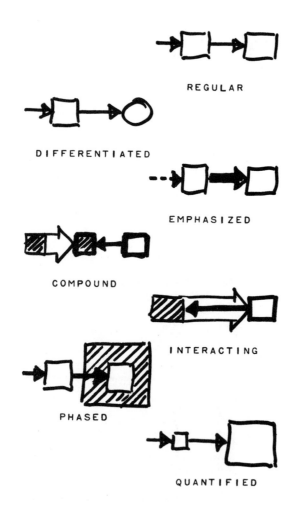

REGULAR

DIFFERENTIATED

EMPHASIZED

COMPOUND

INTERACTING

PHASED

QUANTIFIED

Process concerns the procedure of independent subject actions as a succession of related events. In the graphic figure these actions are summarized in static elements rather than described in active form. Only the procedural steps from element to element are shown to move. Process elements and procedural steps can be *regular* in character, or *differentiated* to express dissimilarities in their varying functions. Major elements in the process can be *emphasized* to indicate their importance. Differentiated element patterns can be organized into a *compound* process or arranged to show an *interacting* process moving in both directions at once. Subject elements can be *phased* in their organization or varied in size as *quantified* process steps. The following figure models represent design solutions to specific problems in these areas.

REGULAR process shows event elements as parallel in meaning. Therefore, basic element forms tend to repeat each other, as do their connecting links. The essential feature of a process figure is its indirect continuity, since it describes a series of separate acts rather than a sustained movement.

FIGURE 1. A simple process showing a regular procedure of elements which are parallel in meaning (see page 40).

FIGURE 2. An interacting process in which elements are treated as circular symbols to permit compositional flexibility.

FIGURE 3. A reverse of the vocabulary of figure 1, that emphasizes the directional links as solid shade forms.

FIGURE 4. Integration of elements and links as common forms for direct association of element meanings.

FIGURE 5. A complex pattern of integrated element-steps differentiated by line and shade into two classes of meaning. Fixed elements are also shown, and are differentiated with respect to their specific meanings.

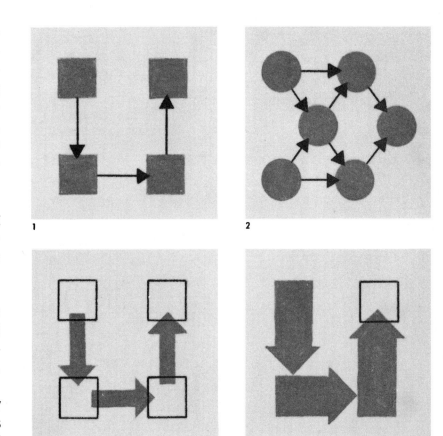

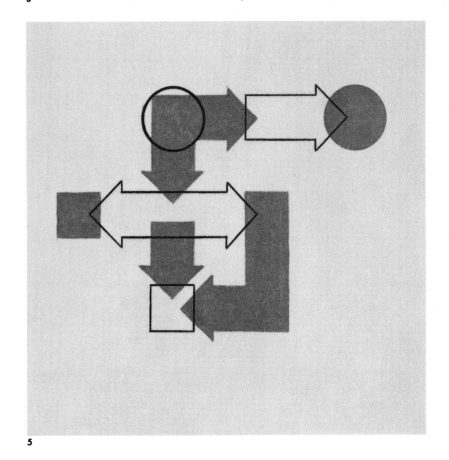

133

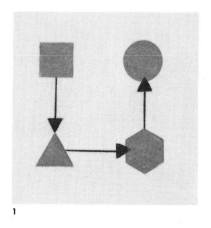

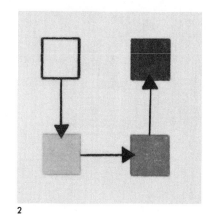

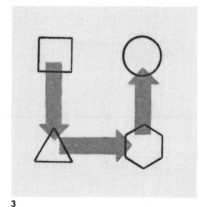

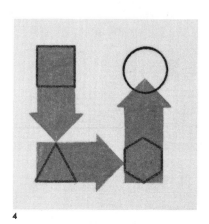

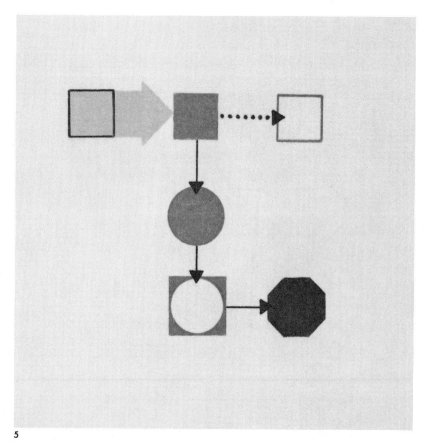

DIFFERENTIATED process elements show differences in meaning through corresponding differences in visual character. Here, visual differentiation is generally achieved through variations in form structure and shade value.

FIGURE 1. A simple process in which element shapes vary to indicate variations in their basic order of meaning.

FIGURE 2. The same process pattern showing varied qualities of meaning within a uniform (square) identity. An order of emphasis is also apparent.

FIGURE 3. The element identities of figure 1 reversed in form to emphasize the process links.

FIGURE 4. The process elements of figure 3 shown in conjunction with integrated element-steps for direct relationship of element contents.

FIGURE 5. A complex process showing a logical procedure of element variations including corresponding changes in link identity when appropriate.

134

EMPHASIZED process steps are shown through differences in the structure and shade value of links, which can create a pattern of relative dominance and subordination in terms of their visual impact and their meaning.

FIGURE 1. A simple process showing increasing emphasis of directional links through line structure.

FIGURE 2. A pattern of increasing emphasis of process links, through darkening shade value. In relation to the outlined element boxes, the links have already been emphasized as solid shapes.

FIGURE 3. Subordination of the final directional link and element, through shade and outline.

FIGURE 4. Emphasis of the initial links of the process, and the concluding element.

FIGURE 5. A system showing a complex order of emphasis and differentiation of directional links, which serves to modify the relative importance of the meaning of each element box.

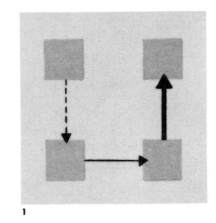

1

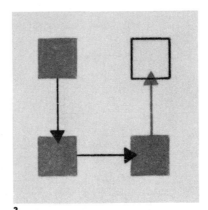

2

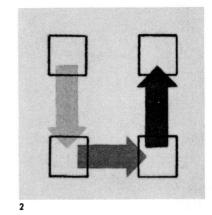

3

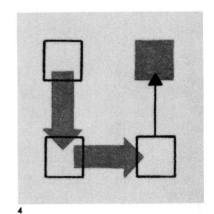

4

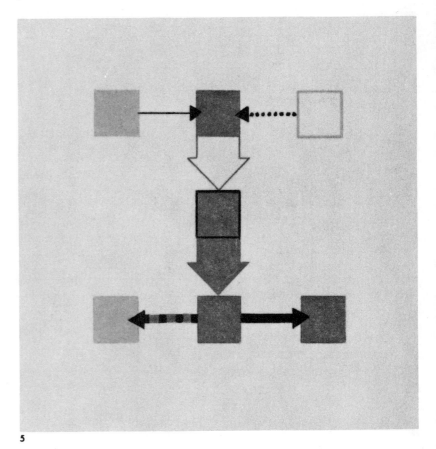

5

135

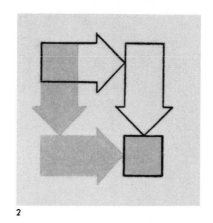

1

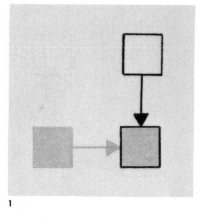

3

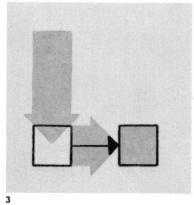

4

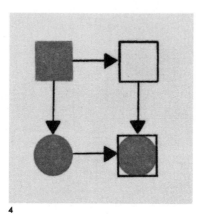

5

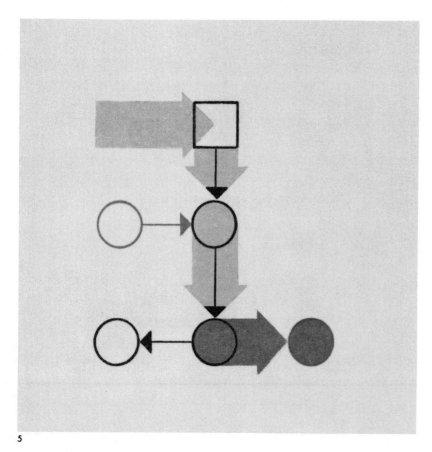

2

COMPOUND process shows a configuration of two or more independent patterns of elements, which act jointly to share certain positions in common. The resulting compound may include joint elements, joint directional links, or both.

FIGURE 1. A compound process in which shaded and linear patterns combine in a concluding element.

FIGURE 2. A compound process of integrated element-steps, utilizing shaded and linear forms which are combined in the beginning and the concluding elements.

FIGURE 3. A process in which the compound pattern is the result of progressive element steps, showing the concluding step as a compound link.

FIGURE 4. A compound process produced by the initial split of element characteristics into two patterns, which combine again to create a reformed element.

FIGURE 5. A compound process in which patterns are differentiated by shade (element-steps) and line (fixed elements and associated links). Relative emphasis of meanings is also evident.

136

INTERACTING process shows a procedure which moves backward as well as forward between elements, creating a reciprocating movement in which the idea pattern returns to its origin. Generally, the return pattern functions in a subordinate role, employing less emphatic form.

FIGURE 1. A simple interaction representing the major process with shaded form and the return pattern with subordinate linear links.

FIGURE 2. A process similar to figure 1 emphasizing the major pattern with unified element-steps.

FIGURE 3. A process in which elements and their related links simultaneously interact in opposite directions.

FIGURE 4. Major and return patterns in a process whose integrated element-steps are differentiated with line and shade.

FIGURE 5. A complex interacting process showing major and return patterns of procedure as well as secondary elements and links, differentiated in their identities.

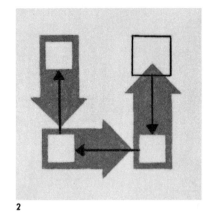

1

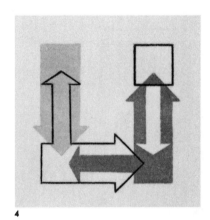

2

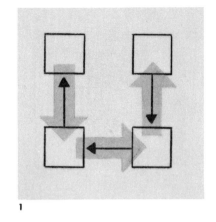

3

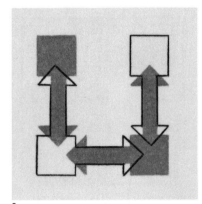

4

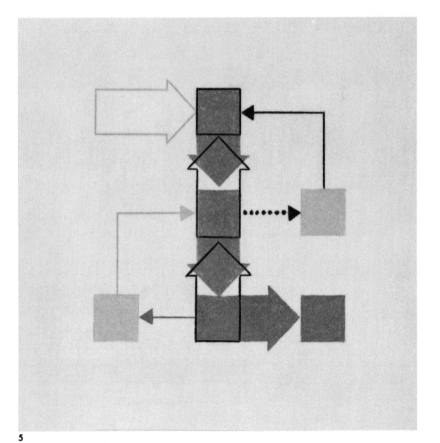

5

137

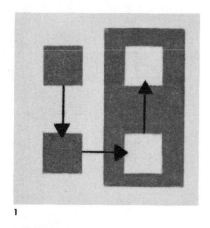

1

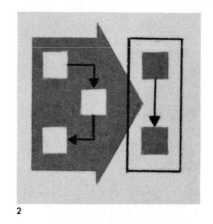

2

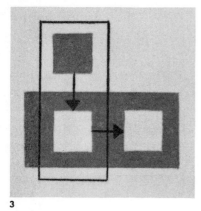

3

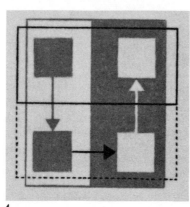

4

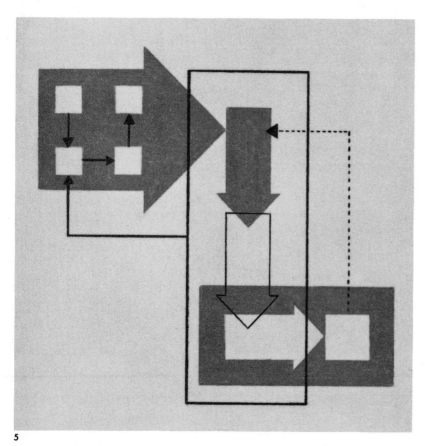

5

PHASED process shows the organization of elements and directional links into functional phases, which generally include both elements and links. Shade reversal and outline are primary means for representing process phases.

FIGURE 1. A simple process showing the concluding elements as a phase with reversed (white) boxes in a shaded area.

FIGURE 2. A process of two phases in which the first pattern as a whole becomes the input for the second.

FIGURE 3. A process of two phases which combine to form a compound at the middle element.

FIGURE 4. A quadruple-phase process showing multiple components in terms of phase organization.

FIGURE 5. A complex process showing three differentiated phases. One acts as a total input, and the others act together as a compound with secondary return links.

QUANTIFIED process shows the relative amount of the subject present in the elements, or the volume of the directional links. Relative distance can also be a quantitative factor in a process pattern. Size, width, and length of forms provide the means for quantitative interpretation.

FIGURE 1. A simple process quantified in terms of element size.

FIGURE 2. A process similar to figure 1 in which quantified elements are shown in circular form for clarity.

FIGURE 3. A process where relative distance between elements is shown to indicate a variable link factor such as time.

FIGURE 4. Quantification of directional links to indicate volume of exchange between elements.

FIGURE 5. A more complex, irregular process pattern which shows quantitative variation in both the elements and the interconnecting links.

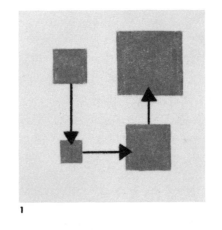

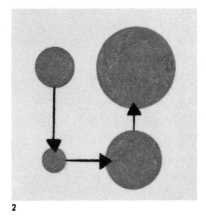

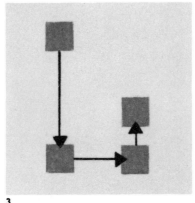

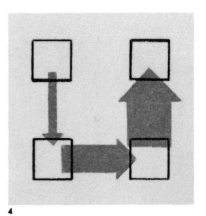

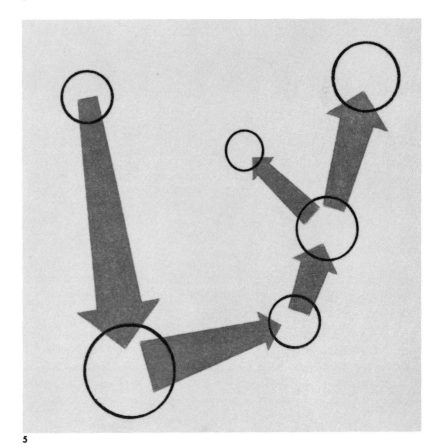

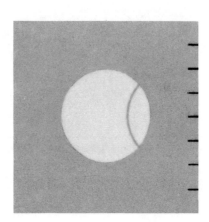

VI

TO SHOW *HOW MUCH*

How much of something there is concerns its physical size, its numerical quantity, its trend of increase or decrease, or the division of its parts in terms of the whole. All four aspects are related in their terms of meaning. Size can show physical quantity; quantity can reflect trend and division; both trend and division can indicate quantity. Nevertheless, in each aspect quantification assumes a different objective, and it is their differing objectives rather than their relationships which make them valuable as communicative approaches. Each takes a different view in showing *how much* of something there is, and widens the range of ideas which can be communicated. Accordingly, size, quantity, trend, and division will be presented here as independent aims, and they will be explored as primary problem areas.

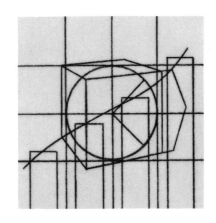

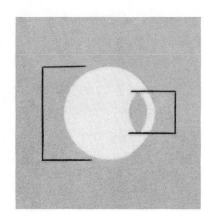

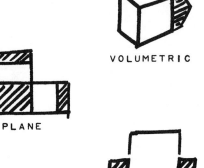

VOLUMETRIC

PLANE

DISTANCE

Size concerns the physical extent of a subject in terms of the space it occupies. In the graphic figure the physical size of a subject element can only be shown relative to that of other elements. Numerical measurements must be introduced if its absolute size is to be stated. Measurement forms can be used to indicate the size of *volumetric* subjects, as well as the size of subjects represented in *plane* form. The size of a space between elements can also be indicated as a *distance* measurement. The following figure models represent design solutions to specific problems in these areas.

VOLUMETRIC size can show the space occupied by a three-dimensional subject, as well as a two-dimensional area or a one-dimensional measurement of one or more of its elements. In all cases the measurement forms, indicating quantitative value, are clearly differentiated from the form of the subject.

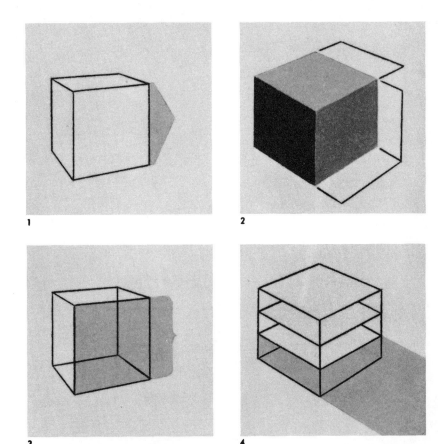

FIGURE 1. The outline of a simple cube object showing a shaded bracket attached to one side to indicate its height (see page 41).

FIGURE 2. A formalized representation of a cube showing three linear brackets to indicate height, width, and depth.

FIGURE 3. The outline cube of figure 1 in which a solid shade indicates the measurement of the entire frontal plane area.

FIGURE 4. A three-level cube subject in which the lower spatial volume is shaded and extended to show a volumetric measurement.

FIGURE 5. A regulator showing linear and diametric measurements extended away from the body area to minimize visual confusion. The regulator is represented in objective form so that its many measured parts can be clearly identified.

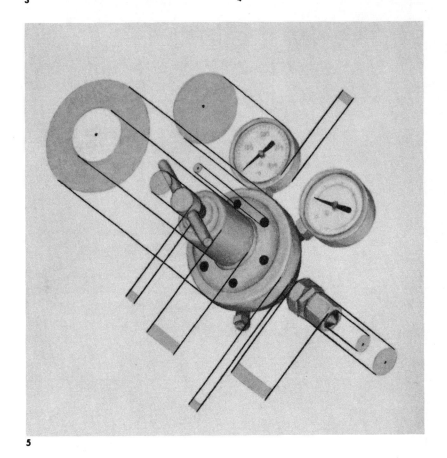

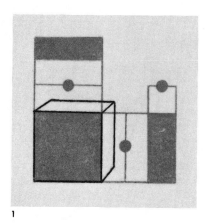

1

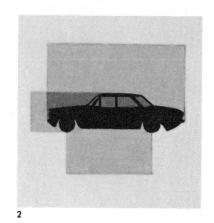

2

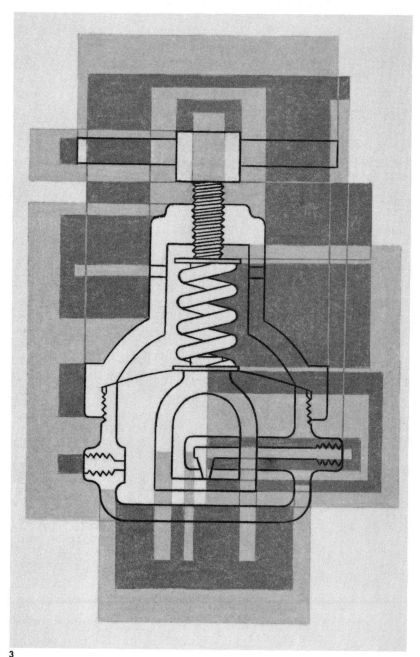

3

PLANE size can show the area of a two-dimensional subject or a one-dimensional measurement of one or more of its elements. Here, as in volumetric subjects, measurement forms are clearly differentiated from the form of the plane subject. While the subject may be volumetric in reality, for this kind of measurement it is translated into, and considered as, plane form.

FIGURE 1. A plane representation (shaded) of a solid object (outline) in which the top and side are shown folded out parallel with the picture plane and measured in relation to the front.

FIGURE 2. An automobile represented in silhouette to facilitate measurement of its height, length, and wheelbase.

FIGURE 3. An outline section view of a regulator showing a complex measurement pattern in which two shades of gray alternate to define the various extensions to be measured. Measurement numbers would appear in each shaded area.

144

DISTANCE size shows the one-dimensional measurement of space between two points or subjects. While the measurement itself is a one-dimensional extension, a subject's distance from each of several others can be shown simultaneously with several measurement extensions, giving it a specific two-dimensional location.

FIGURE 1. A simple measurement of the distances between three objects.

FIGURE 2. A symbolic measurement, from a fixed scale, of the relative altitudes of three different aircraft.

FIGURE 3. A distance measurement, from a concentric scale, of three objects from a common center point.

FIGURE 4. Horizontal and vertical measurement, from a coordinate grid scale, of four elements to show plane location. Each element location represents the intersection of two independent distance measurements.

FIGURE 5. A road network and associated place locations showing the distances (shaded) between each of several places and a central place.

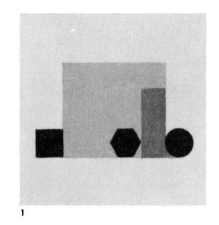
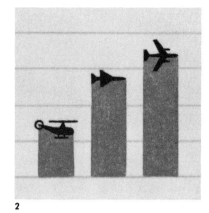
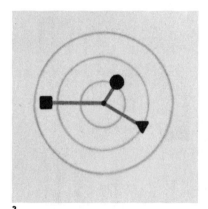
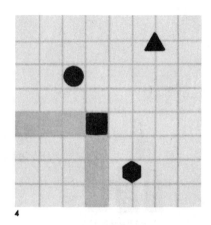
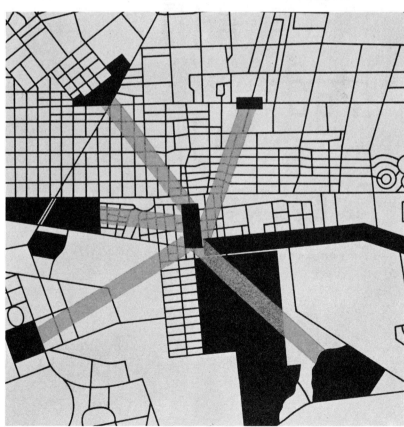

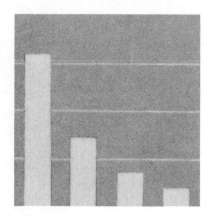

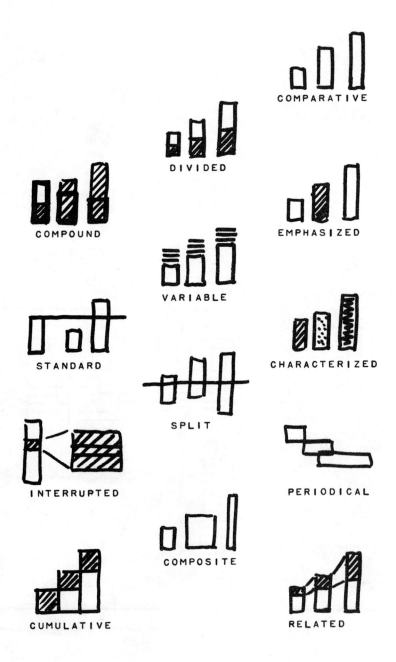

COMPARATIVE

DIVIDED

COMPOUND

EMPHASIZED

VARIABLE

STANDARD

CHARACTERIZED

SPLIT

INTERRUPTED

PERIODICAL

COMPOSITE

CUMULATIVE

RELATED

Quantity concerns the amount of a subject in terms of a fixed scale of measure. In the graphic figure, quantity can be shown in *comparative* relation to other quantities, through the extension of abstract parallel bar forms. The height of each bar form is measured in terms of a common scale, and corresponds to the quantity of the subject. The bars themselves can show *divided* quantities, or differentiated groups of quantities in a *compound* arrangement. A specific quantity can be *emphasized* or shown as a *variable* amount. Quantities can also be shown in terms of a *standard* amount, or visually *characterized* in relation to the subjects they represent. Bar elements can be organized on a *split* scale, to show opposing quantities, or be represented as *periodical* in relation to time. Bar elements can be *interrupted* to show a detailed enlargement of a quantity, or to omit an unnecessary bar segment. Bar elements can be scaled in width as well as height, to show amounts which are a *composite* of two quantitative factors. Quantities can also be shown as *cumulative,* or as *related* in their progression. The following figure models represent design solutions to specific problems in these areas.

146

COMPARATIVE quantity shows the amount of a subject in direct visual relation to other subject amounts, through the use of extended bar forms whose heights correspond to subject quantities. This type of figure is often termed a "bar" chart. The bars are measured in terms of a common scale, which is generally represented as a subordinate frame of reference.

FIGURE 1. A simple representation of four amounts, shown in close proximity to facilitate comparison (see page 42).

FIGURE 2. A horizontal version of the bars of figure 1, to enable efficient placement of lengthy word identifications whose horizontality would be difficult to associate with vertical bars.

FIGURE 3. A series of many comparative amounts represented in linear form to emphasize continuity rather than separation.

FIGURE 4. Four amounts shown connected to indicate the progressive quantification of a single subject identity.

FIGURE 5. A more complex example of related amounts associated with a single subject, but finely divided to individualize each amount.

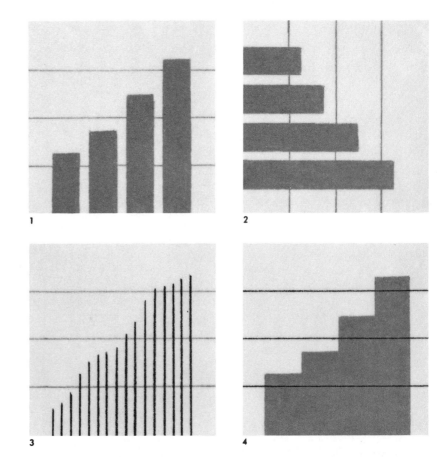

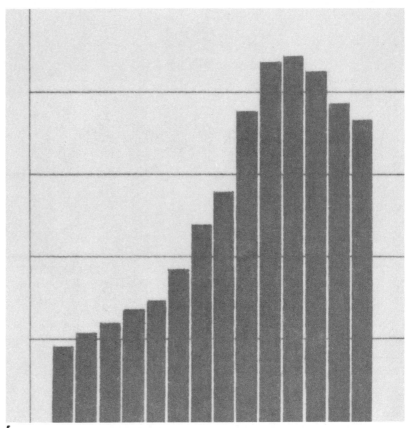

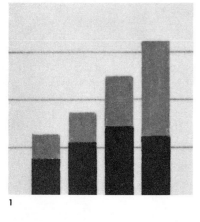
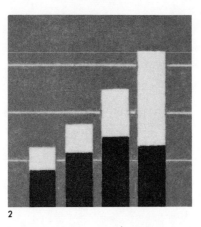

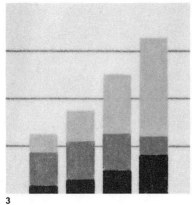
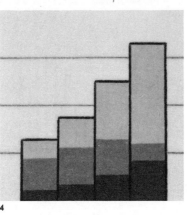

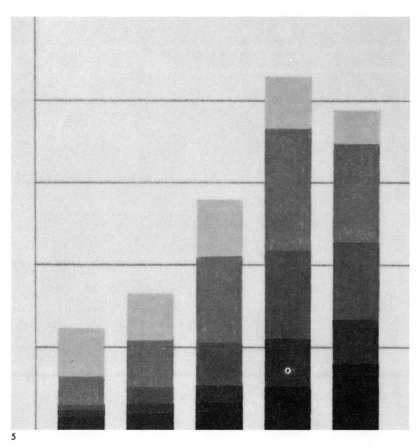

DIVIDED quantity shows a subject amount whose representative bar is split into two or more component segments that indicate fractional amounts of the whole. In each bar, the segment amounts are additive. As forms, the divided amounts require visual differentiation usually achieved through varying shade values.

FIGURE 1. A simple divided quantity using black and gray for element differentiation.

FIGURE 2. A reversal of the gray and white pattern of figure 1, to maximize differentiation (as black and white) between component elements of each bar.

FIGURE 3. A triple division of amounts using two gray values and black.

FIGURE 4. A triple division of progressive amounts in which a black outline is used to separate each amount.

FIGURE 5. Multiple division of progressive amounts using shade value differentiation. For more than this number of divisions, shade value differences become difficult to distinguish, and other means for differentiation should be sought (see page 153).

COMPOUND quantity shows two or more progressions of subject amounts concurrently. Each bar group represents two or more distinct quantities which are comparative rather than additive. In practice, they can represent different occasions of measure of a single subject's quantity.

FIGURE 1. A series of compound quantities superimposed and differentiated by outline and solid shade.

FIGURE 2. A large series of compound quantities shown as narrow bars to emphasize group continuity rather than individual identity.

FIGURE 3. Compound quantities shown through parallel arrangement in which each pair represents two occasions of measure of a subject less related than in figure 1.

FIGURE 4. Compound pairs of amounts in which each pair is measured in terms of the same two occasions.

FIGURE 5. A quadruple compound in which each successive subject is measured in terms of four standard occasions.

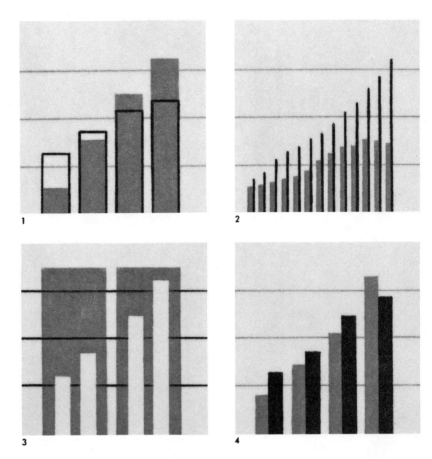

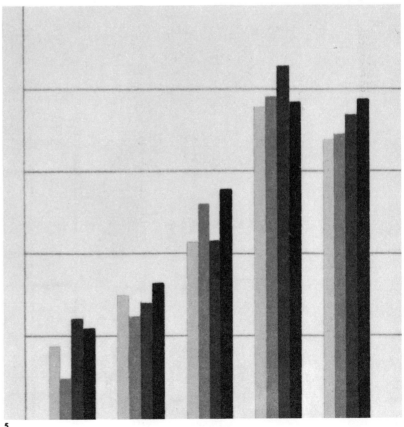

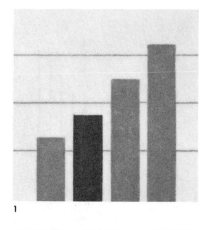

1

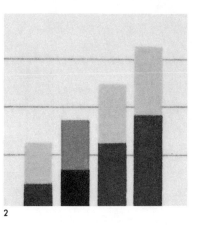

2

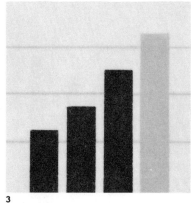

3

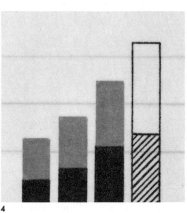

4

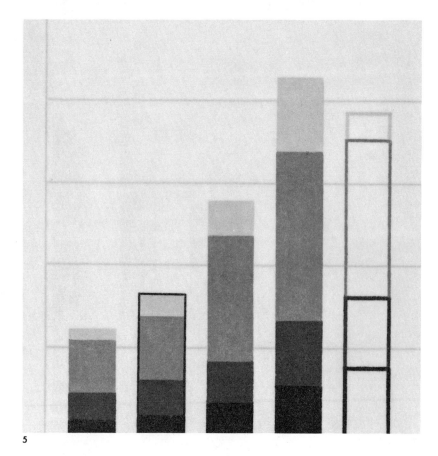

5

EMPHASIZED quantity shows the particular importance of one amount in relation to neighboring amounts. If all but one of the quantities are visually emphasized, that one becomes correspondingly subordinate in character, and can indicate indefinite meanings such as estimated or projected quantity.

FIGURE 1. The emphasis of one quantity in a series, through darker value.

FIGURE 2. The emphasis of a divided quantity in a series, through a relative darkening of the values of both quantity components.

FIGURE 3. The subordination of the last quantity in a series to suggest probable quantity, by emphasizing the first three quantities.

FIGURE 4. The subordination of the last quantity in a series by giving it a weaker line form, to indicate a planned or projected quantity.

FIGURE 5. A complex series of divided quantities in which the second amount is emphasized by a reinforcing outline, and the last amount is subordinated by outline alone.

VARIABLE quantity shows a generalized amount whose exact numerical measurement is not determined. The amount represented can vary from a minimum to a maximum, indicate a possible median, suggest a probable quantity with a possible range of error, or simply fade out visually in direct relation to its decreasing probability.

FIGURE 1. A series of quantities which show maximum and minimum limits and also indicate decreasing probability through form disintegration.

FIGURE 2. A series of estimated quantities showing also a probable range of variation with fixed limits.

FIGURE 3. A series of probable quantities and a suggestion of possible variation upward.

FIGURE 4. A series of quantities whose range of variation is used to make an angular cut which suggests the degree of variability.

FIGURE 5. A series of quantities, each with a defined maximum limit of variability, but an undefined lower limit which is shown by graduated shading.

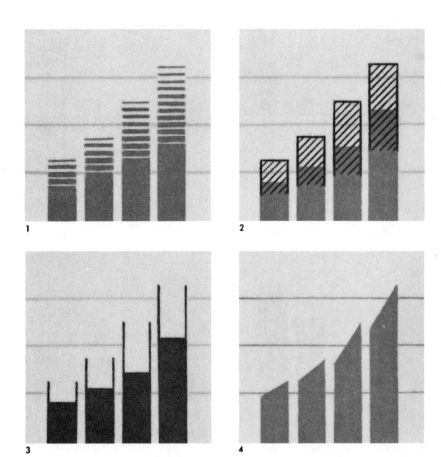

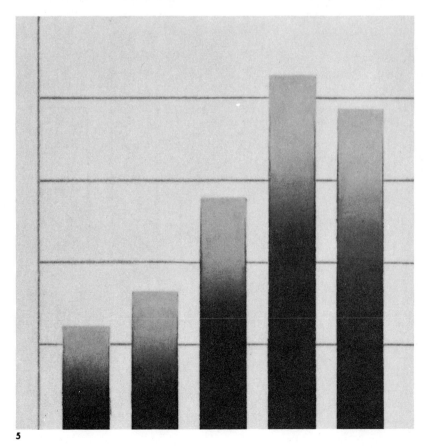

151

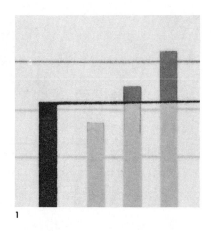

1

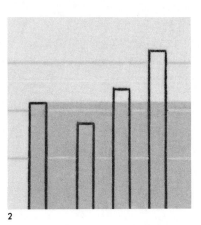

2

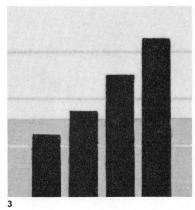

3

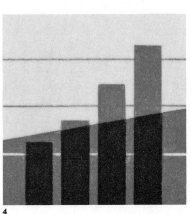

4

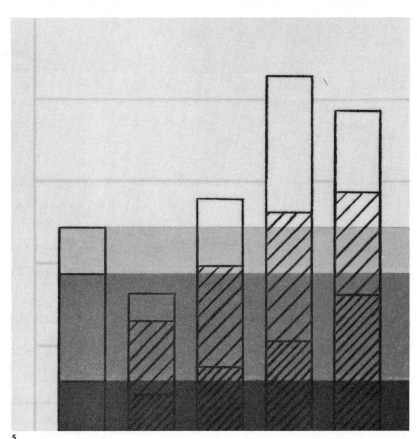

5

STANDARD quantity shows a series of different amounts in terms of one fixed amount, which serves as a basic criterion for the evaluation of the others. This means that any bar quantity which does not equal the standard quantity is seen as either excessive or deficient, since it varies from the ordinate standard line projected by the fixed amount.

FIGURE 1. A standard quantity, as black, in relation to three gray quantities which are darkened for emphasis when they exceed the standard line.

FIGURE 2. A standard quantity emphasized by a shaded area in relation to subordinated outline bars.

FIGURE 3. A standard quantity shown without a standard bar as a subordinate frame of reference for emphatic black quantities.

FIGURE 4. An increasing standard quantity which acts to emphasize (as black) the segments of the bar quantities which it includes.

FIGURE 5. A complex version of figure 2 showing divided quantities (line) as well as a corresponding divided standard (gray).

CHARACTERIZED quantity shows differentiated bar identity through differentiated structure, shade value, and texture. Frequently, form characteristics require assigned meanings to act as temporary conventional symbols. At other times, associative features serve to identify the subject meanings.

FIGURE 1. Differentiated shade character designating individual bar identities which decrease in visual importance as they increase in quantity.

FIGURE 2. Characterized bar divisions, using shade, line, and texture to maximize identity differentiation at the expense of the visual unity of the whole.

FIGURE 3. Dramatic characterization of closely related bar quantities which act as individual linear symbols.

FIGURE 4. Characterization of quantities as a whole through subject association.

FIGURE 5. Symbolic characterization of quantified substances through texture, using shade value to identify divided amounts within each bar.

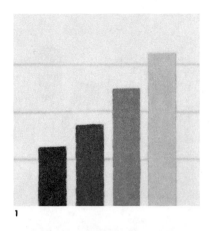

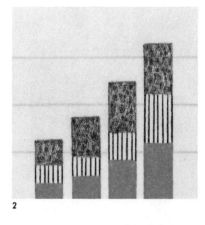

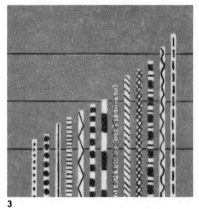

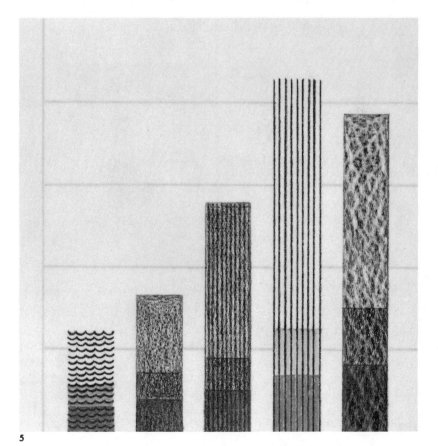

153

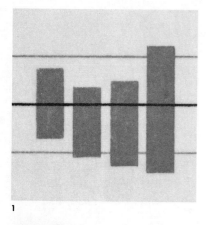

1

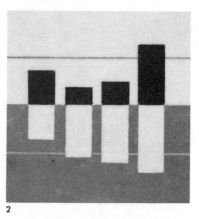

2

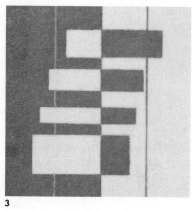

3

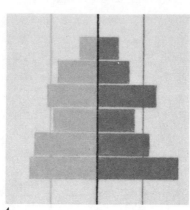

4

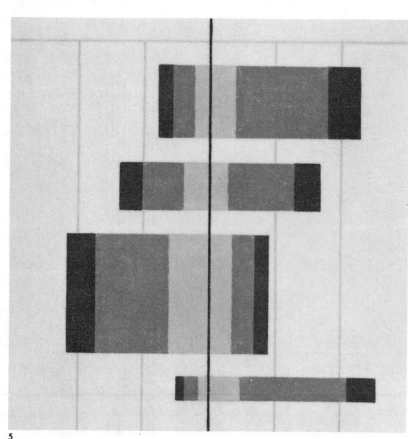

5

SPLIT quantity shows an amount in relation to a dividing line which separates the whole amount into two areas of quantitative measure. The two areas are mutually complimentary, and they serve to create a divided quantity in which each amount is measured on an individual scale that begins on the dividing line and proceeds outward in both directions. Split quantity can show positive and negative conditions, or other dual measures of a subject.

FIGURE 1. Simple split quantity in which subject unity is maintained as continuous gray bar form.

FIGURE 2. Split quantity in which positive and negative aspects are differentiated as black and white.

FIGURE 3. Split percentages of related wholes quantified in width and shown on a vertical dividing line to permit interior, horizontal bar identification.

FIGURE 4. Dual aspects of a split quantity in which individual bars are shown to be closely related in subject meaning.

FIGURE 5. A complex example of split quantity in which each of the dual aspects is subdivided into fractional amounts of a fixed whole, and quantified specifically in terms of bar width.

154

PERIODICAL quantity shows the amount or extent of a subject element relative to a measured continuum, such as time, in which the element is represented as a quantitative span within that continuum. A related grouping of periodical bar elements can create a sequential pattern which shows the measured phasing of a subject.

FIGURE 1. A simple pattern of periodical phases in which each element begins at the termination of the preceding element.

FIGURE 2. A pattern of periods, each with a subordinate subdivision which acts as an overlapping period. Increasing shade value indicates phase progression.

FIGURE 3. An overlapping periodical pattern shown in terms of specific phase areas (gray values).

FIGURE 4. Periodical quantities shown in terms of beginning (shade) and terminating (outline/shade) measurements.

FIGURE 5. A complex periodical pattern showing differentiated (outline/shade) phases and tapered elements to indicate gradual beginning and termination.

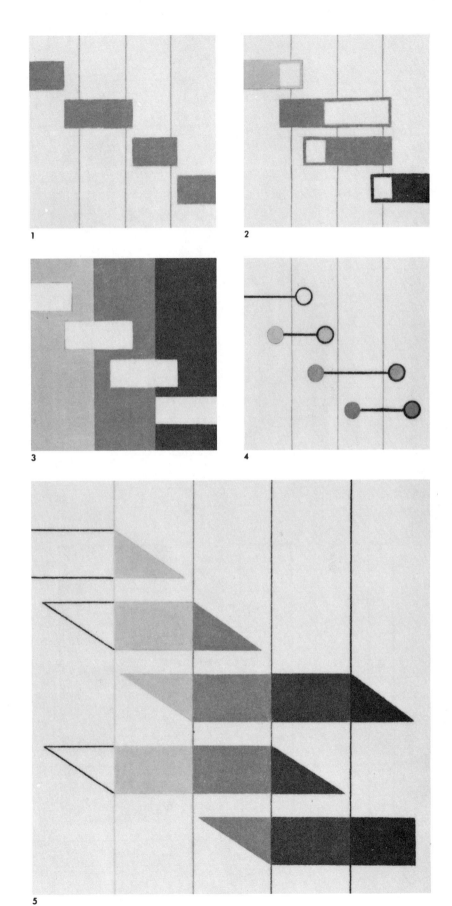

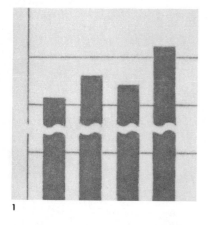

1

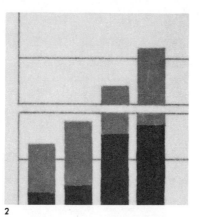

2

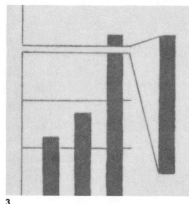

3

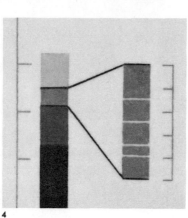

4

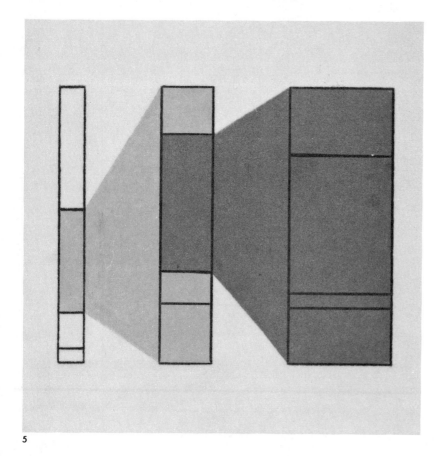

5

INTERRUPTED quantity is where the measured amount is broken in form and/or scale to omit unnecessary segments or to enlarge important ones for detailed description of its components. While omission interruptions serve the visual economy of the figure, enlargement interruptions serve its visual clarity in representing small amounts.

FIGURE 1. The removal of a central area from a series of very similar quantities, to permit a scale for bar differentiation that would otherwise be too tall to be manageable.

FIGURE 2. An interrupted scale, clearly defined so that only the last two quantities appear broken. Here, the interruption is used to accommodate widely differing amounts within an economical image.

FIGURE 3. An interrupted large quantity in which the removed segment is visually represented for reference.

FIGURE 4. An enlargement of a quantity segment to show its subdivided amounts.

FIGURE 5. A double enlargement to show multiple levels of detail in one element of a quantified subject.

COMPOSITE quantity is shown as a product of two separate numerical factors. In plane form, it is represented by a rectangular shape whose height shows one quantitative factor while its width shows the other. The area created represents the total quantity as quantity per unit multiplied by number of units.

FIGURE 1. A series of composite quantities similar in area totals but varying in height and width factors.

FIGURE 2. Composite quantities in which the vertical factor represents percentage of a whole.

FIGURE 3. Composite quantities in which divisional variations in quantity are shown in terms of standard vertical percentage.

FIGURE 4. A composite quantity in a two-dimensional whole showing divisional percentage in terms of two scaled factors.

FIGURE 5. A complex version of figure 4 in which the vertical scale factor is also variable rather than constant.

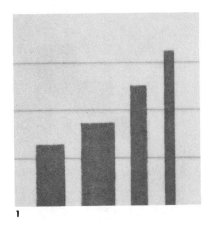

1

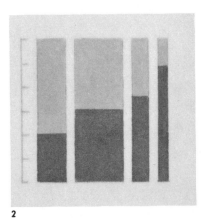

2

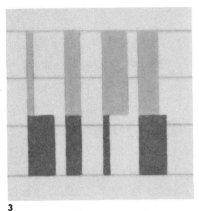

3

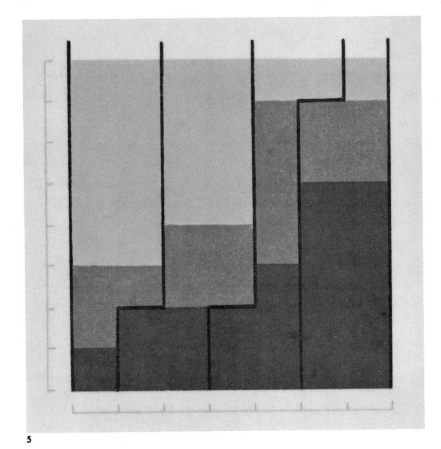

4

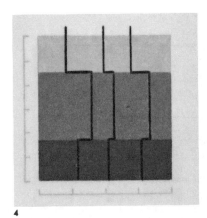

5

1

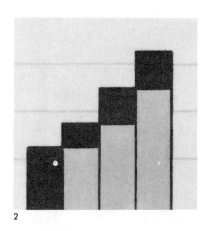

2

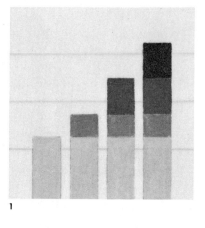

3

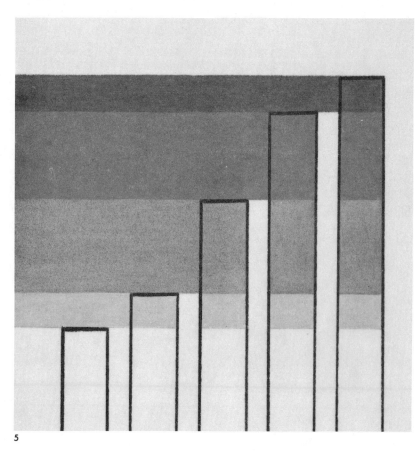

4

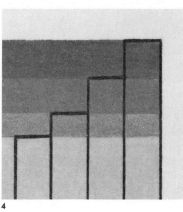

5

CUMULATIVE quantity shows the progressive increase of an amount through incremental additions. In representing each cumulative element, the previous total is brought forward as the base quantity and is added to the amount of increase for that occasion.

FIGURE 1. A series of cumulative amounts in which each additional amount is differentiated by shade value, to maintain its identity throughout.

FIGURE 2. Cumulative increases emphasized as black and joined for continuity.

FIGURE 3. The cumulative pattern of figure 2 showing ordinate guidelines for direct measurement and representing only the increases.

FIGURE 4. Cumulative increase shown as subordinate description of total quantity bars and related directly to the ordinate scale.

FIGURE 5. A modified version of figure 4 in which bars are spaced to separate and identify the cumulative components. Gray values differentiate each successive addition.

158

RELATED quantity is where the relationship between varying amounts is visually identified and represented as a directional increase, decrease, or trend. Form differentiation is essential to separate actual quantities from their generalized trend patterns.

FIGURE 1. Related outline quantities in which upper and lower measurements are connected and the divisional area between emphasized as a solid shade.

FIGURE 2. The quantities of figure 1 emphasizing the non-related amounts as black and unifying the related segments with gray line and shade.

FIGURE 3. The same quantities in which the trends of the divisional amounts are generalized by curves.

FIGURE 4. Concentrated linear quantity bars whose averaged trend is indicated by an emphatic gray curve.

FIGURE 5. A complex version of figure 2 in which multiple quantity divisions are related by connecting lines of corresponding gray values.

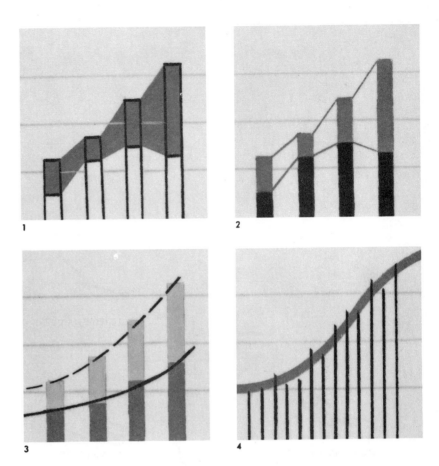

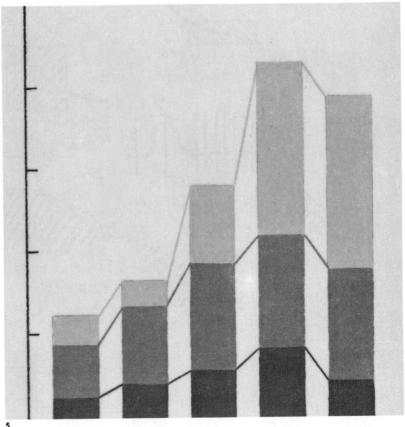

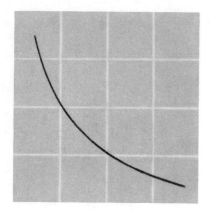

3
TREND

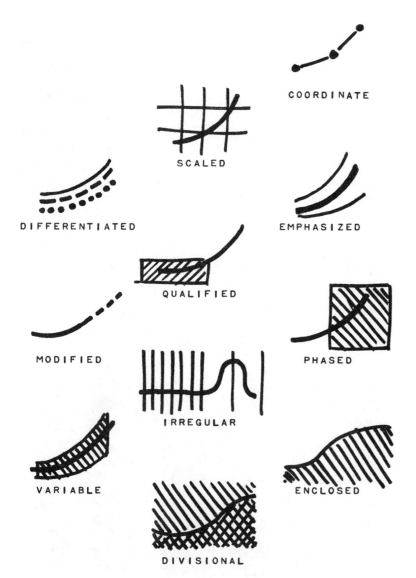

COORDINATE

SCALED

DIFFERENTIATED

EMPHASIZED

QUALIFIED

MODIFIED

PHASED

IRREGULAR

VARIABLE

ENCLOSED

DIVISIONAL

Trend concerns the progressive increase or decrease of a subject in terms of its amount. In the graphic figure, trend can be shown as a succession of abstract *coordinate* points whose locations are determined by intersecting numerical values. The trend, itself, can be represented by connecting lines or by a generalized curve. To define its quantitative meaning, the trend pattern is *scaled* by a grid structure. The curve can be *differentiated* or *emphasized* through its own linear character. A trend segment can be *qualified* in meaning by a coordinate area, or it can be *modified* in structure to represent such ideas as projected trend. The trend line can be shown in terms of a *phased* quantitative progression, or its grid scale can be modified to accommodate *irregular* curve fluctuations. The curve can be widened to show *variable* trend. It can also be shown as an *enclosed* area or as a variable border line, to indicate the *divisional* trend within a whole quantity. The following figure models represent design solutions to specific problems in these areas.

COORDINATE trend shows a related sequence of quantities, represented as points, whose exact locations are determined by intersecting numerical values projected from the ordinate (vertical) and abscissa (horizontal) sides of a coordinate grid scale. Point sequences can be connected to describe the trend of the coordinate values. This type of figure is known as a "graph".

FIGURE 1. A representation of the coordinate areas defined by a succession of coordinate points.

FIGURE 2. The points of figure 1 connected to show trend sequences.

FIGURE 3. Value ranges between corresponding points in two sequences.

FIGURE 4. Identification (gray shade) of an area of importance between two pairs of coordinate points.

FIGURE 5. Three differentiated trends connected for continuity.

FIGURE 6. The trend pattern of figure 5 using grays to differentiate points as parts of a related subject.

FIGURE 7. Three connected trends, differentiated with gray values.

FIGURE 8. The trends of figure 7 in which curve lines are used to generalize their directions and emphasize their continuity.

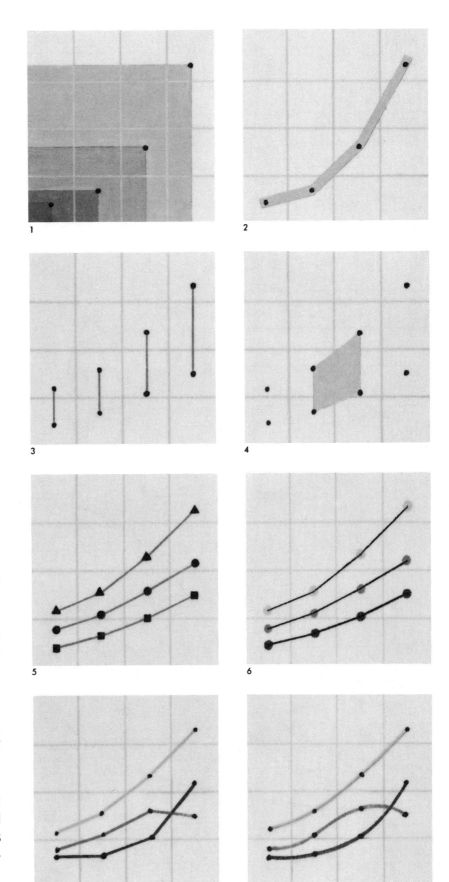

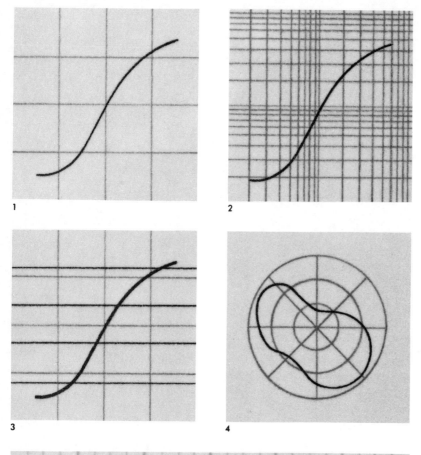

SCALED trend defines the quantitative meaning of the curve through its grid structure, which acts as a subordinate frame of reference for estimating the quantitative progress of the curve. While all trends are scaled for meaning, the character of that meaning can vary with the structure of the scale itself, which can represent any orderly progression of magnitudes.

FIGURE 1. A regular progression of grid scale intervals subordinated as gray lines.

FIGURE 2. A double logarithmic grid which defines the trend curve in terms of a regularly decreasing scale of quantity, represented in cycles of ten units each. Logarithmic grids can be used to represent rapid increases or decreases.

FIGURE 3. A compound ordinate scale in which black and gray grid lines represent different terms of measure for the same curve.

FIGURE 4. A concentric scale used to represent cyclical trends.

FIGURE 5. A regular grid scale progression showing fine-line subdivisions for detailed trend measurement.

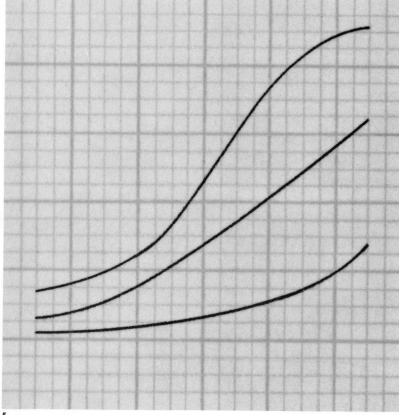

DIFFERENTIATED trend character shows the identity of the various curves and serves to distinguish them from one another. Visual differentiation can be created through linear width, shade value, and textural pattern.

FIGURE 1. Three simple curves differentiated in width to indicate dissimilar identity and order of importance.

FIGURE 2. Three curves differentiated in structure but similar in importance through balance in line weight.

FIGURE 3. Differentiated identity and an order of importance, as in figure 1, but through shade value to suggest variations of a related subject.

FIGURE 4. Differentiated curves characterized as symbolic compounds of simple forms.

FIGURE 5. A complex pattern of trend curves differentiated in a variety of ways to permit clear identification of each curve, particularly those which coincide and would otherwise merge visually as a single curve.

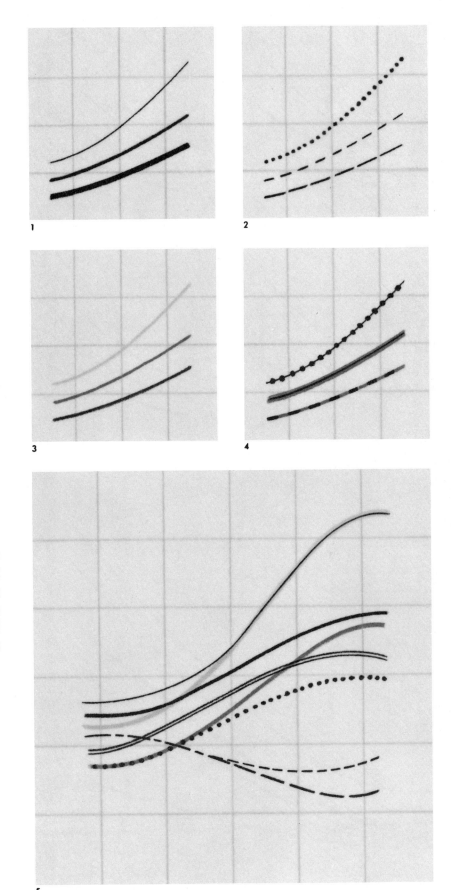

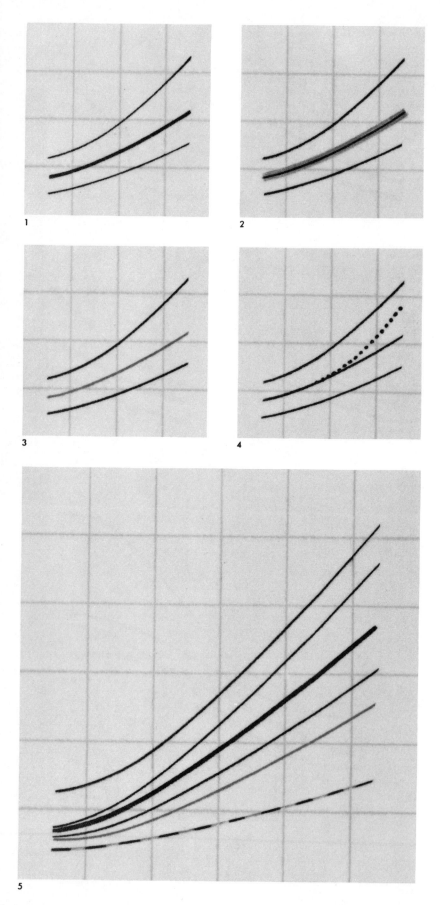

EMPHASIZED trend through its visual dominance shows the relative importance of one curve in relation to another. Conversely, the emphasis of all but one curve automatically assigns that curve a subordinate role. Visual emphasis can be achieved through linear width and darkness, as subordination can be achieved through thinner and lighter form.

FIGURE 1. Three simple trends in which the middle curve is emphasized by greater line width.

FIGURE 2. The same curves showing emphasis by reinforcing the middle curve with a wider gray shade which permits curve structures and their visual meanings to remain similar.

FIGURE 3. Three trends, the middle one subordinated by a gray value.

FIGURE 4. Three equal trends with a dotted secondary (subordinate) curve separating from the center trend.

FIGURE 5. A group of trends whose varying form characteristics create an order of relative emphasis.

QUALIFIED trend shows a curve element in relation to a defined area of coordinate meaning, which derives from an intersection of coordinate value lines of designated meaning with a specific point on the curve. The part of the curve included by the resultant area is qualified by the designated meaning of the area.

FIGURE 1. Two areas of qualified trend differentiated by light and medium shade values.

FIGURE 2. An area defined by two abscissa values related to the trend only, to qualify its meaning.

FIGURE 3. A single designated abscissa value related to two trend quantities to produce two areas of qualified meaning.

FIGURE 4. An area defined by two abscissa values and related to the space between two curves, as an area of qualified meaning.

FIGURE 5. Two areas of qualified meaning defined by two abscissa values related to two trends, whose intersected quantities are indicated by dashed lines.

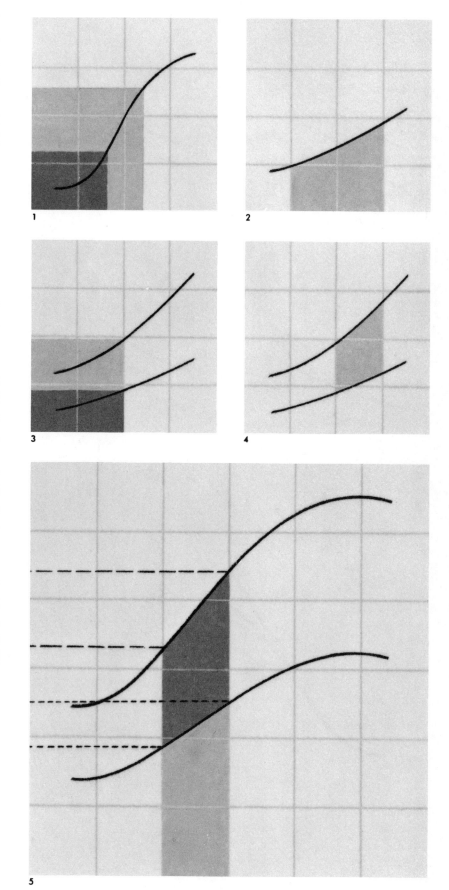

165

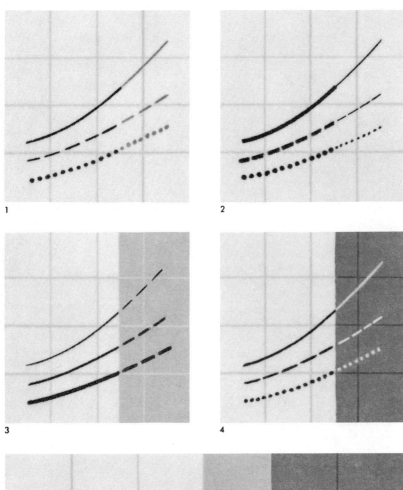

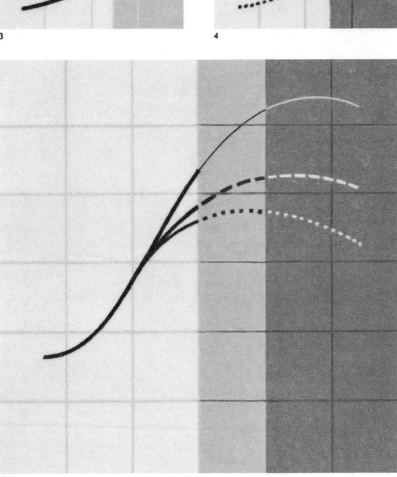

MODIFIED trend shows a curve structure which changes character at a specific abscissa value to reflect a change in the nature or quality of the subsequent values. Modified curve structure is often used to represent estimated or projected trends, in which case the structure is visually subordinated.

FIGURE 1. Three differentiated curves showing estimated trends through subordinated gray line segments.

FIGURE 2. Similar curves representing projected trends by reduced (subordinated) line width.

FIGURE 3. Three curves in an order of emphasis, showing projected trends by dashed lines and identifying the area of projection with a solid shade.

FIGURE 4. Three curves (as in figure 1) showing estimated trends within an identified dark shade area which permits white line structure.

FIGURE 5. A composite of elements from figures 3 and 4, showing two areas of anticipated trends for three curves deriving from a common trend.

PHASED trend shows curve elements in relation to independent areas of coordinate meaning. While such areas are generally associated with progressive abscissa values, they can also be shown as ordinate phases. Phases can be identified by scale lines or by the areas between, using shades of gray in either case for visual differentiation.

FIGURE 1. A coordinate trend area of three independent phases differentiated by varying shades of gray.

FIGURE 2. Three independent phases defined by differentiated gray grid lines.

FIGURE 3. A trend area of two phases, the second of which is graduated in its shading to indicate gradual change in meaning.

FIGURE 4. A trend area of two ordinate phases which apply to the variable curve quantities.

FIGURE 5. A complex coordinate phase pattern which includes three progressive abscissa phases (light to dark) that are divided horizontally into two ordinate phases (line and shade).

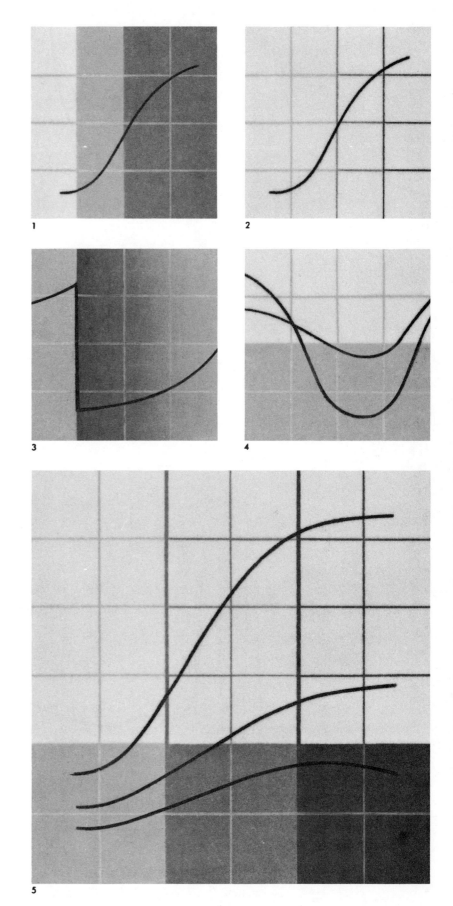

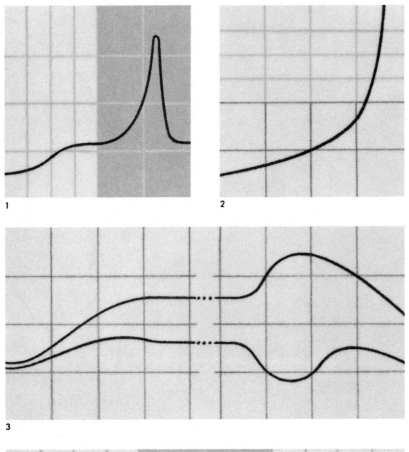

IRREGULAR trend shows a curve pattern which fluctuates considerably in its overall character and requires scale enlargement or omission of segments in order to represent the nature of the trend as an efficient image.

FIGURE 1. An enlarged scale area showing clearly the sharp peak formed by the trend curve.

FIGURE 2. An enlarged lower scale area showing in detail the part of the curve which increases gradually.

FIGURE 3. A removed center scale area omitting an unchanging trend segment and relating the segments which vary.

FIGURE 4. A complex irregular curve where the central scale progression is enlarged to permit detailed definition of the trend peaks and valley, and where the ordinate scale is broken to omit long segments of continuous vertical trend.

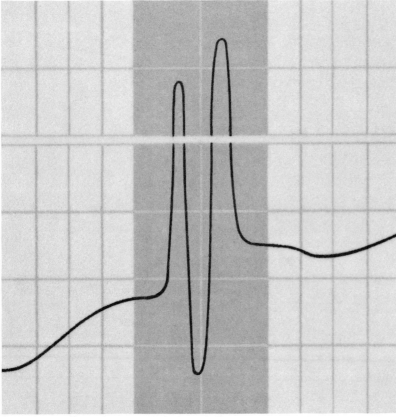

VARIABLE trend shows a curve structure which is widened to indicate a range in its quantitative value. This variability can express areas of possible deviation from a probable median curve or areas of possibility between two curves representing the extreme cases of the trend. Generally, the area of variability is shaded.

FIGURE 1. Two variable trend areas showing a curve line in the lower example to indicate the range of possible variability from a designated curve.

FIGURE 2. Two examples of graduated trend probability, the lower one including a defined probability curve.

FIGURE 3. Two line curves which represent extreme cases of variation for a trend which could occur anywhere in the shaded area between them.

FIGURE 4. Intersecting curve extremes which define each of the two areas between them as areas of variability.

FIGURE 5. A complex grouping of curves from which is generalized an area of trend probability (dark shade) and two outer areas of possibility (light shade).

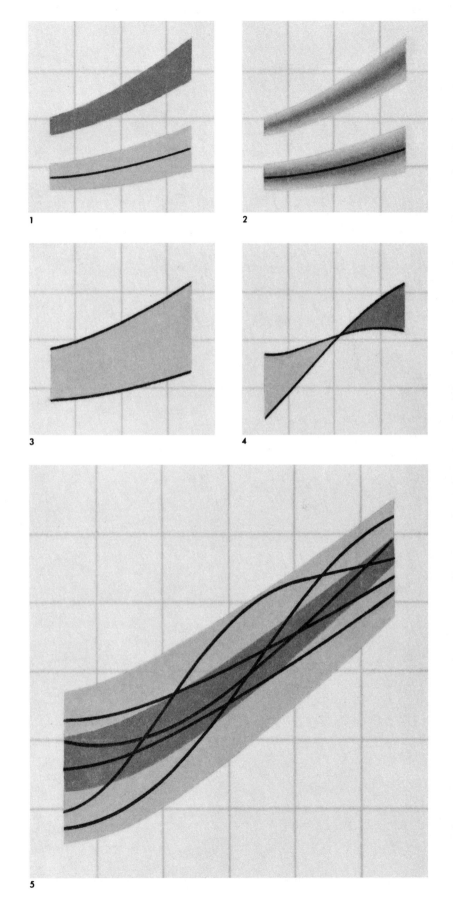

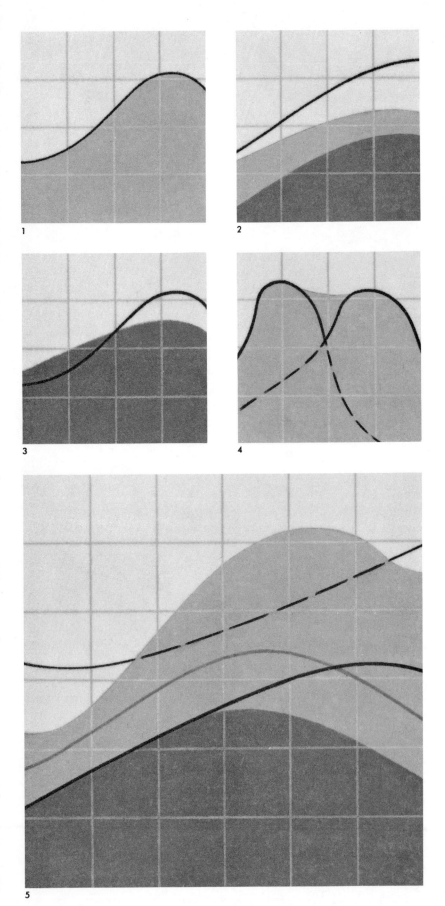

ENCLOSED trend shows a curve that is created or reinforced by a solid form extending to the floor and adjacent walls of the grid, to identify the quantitative area contained by the curve as well as its trend. In this role it acts as an irregular area of coordinate meaning and is usually represented by a gray shade.

FIGURE 1. A simple trend line reinforced by a solid shade which encloses the quantitative area defined by the curve to emphasize its cumulative substance.

FIGURE 2. Two enclosed trends, defined as substances, and an independent curve not representing an enclosed trend.

FIGURE 3. An intersection of an independent trend with an enclosed, cumulative trend area.

FIGURE 4. The intersection of two curves whose combined trend is identified as a shaded area and includes a trend rationalization of the space between the two peaks.

FIGURE 5. A complex trend pattern in which three differentiated trends are shown in relation to two enclosed trend areas.

DIVISIONAL trend shows the separation of a whole amount in relation to trends of quantitative measure. Each part of the whole is represented as a fractional area and can be identified by line, shade, or both. This type of figure is often used to show the division of a whole in terms of time.

FIGURE 1. A simple divisional trend showing three components by differentiated shade values.

FIGURE 2. Four divisional trend areas whose separating curves are identified (as line) and are shown independently as anticipated dividing lines.

FIGURE 3. A divisional trend of four components whose fluctuations are represented by straight connections within emphasized abscissa intervals.

FIGURE 4. A compound divisional trend which includes an overlapping component and a secondary alternative trend curve, as well as four basic areas of division.

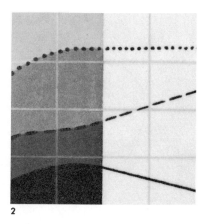
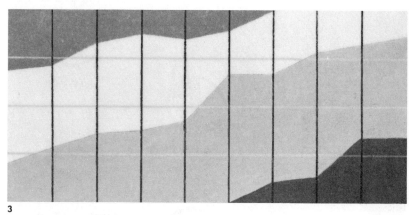
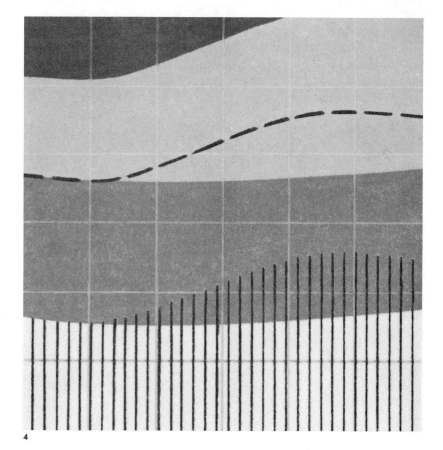

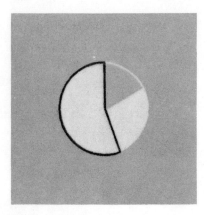

DIFFERENTIATED

UNIFIED

GROUPED

EMPHASIZED

COMPOUND

VARIABLE

EXTENDED

Division concerns the separation of a whole amount in terms of its component quantities. In the graphic figure, a circular form can be used to represent a whole amount, and can be divided into segments which represent proportional quantities, or percentages, of the whole. The segments can be related in character to create a visually *unified* whole, or *differentiated* in character to distinguish each element. An important segment can be *emphasized,* or several related segments can be *grouped* together. *Variable* dividing lines can also be represented. Division segments can be combined into a *compound* relationship, or *extended* radially as specific amounts in addition to being divided circumferentially. The following figure models represent design solutions to specific problems in these areas.

UNIFIED division shows separated percentage segments in relation to a visually unified whole, to emphasize the singleness or continuity of the subject represented. Here, total relationship of the form is important.

FIGURE 1. A simple division of a whole amount in which the amount as a whole is distinguished by a solid shade (see page 44).

FIGURE 2. A division in which the segment lines are extended beyond the rim of the subordinated whole to permit detailed description.

FIGURE 3. An emphatic description of participating segments to indicate the individual inputs to the unified whole.

FIGURE 4. The division of a financial quantity symbolized by a separated coin which, as such, also conveys a unified identity to the whole amount.

FIGURE 5. A combined version of figures 1 and 2 showing a unified (shaded) whole which is divided into extended segments for external identification.

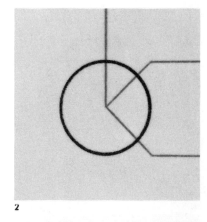

1

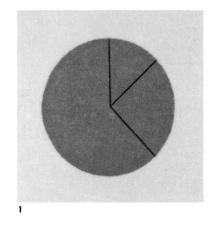

2

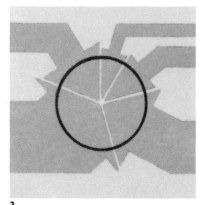

3

4

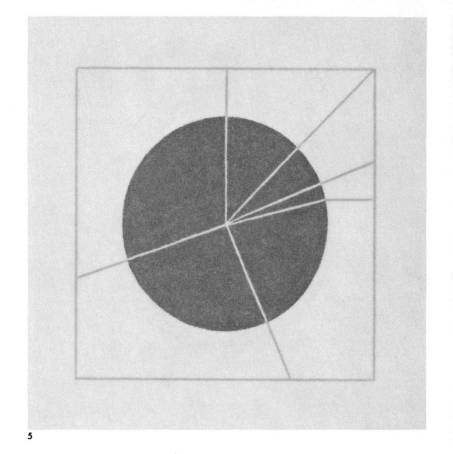

5

173

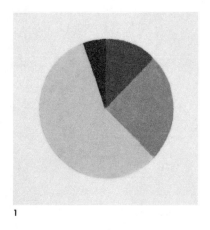

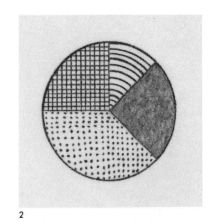

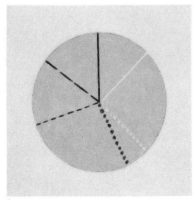

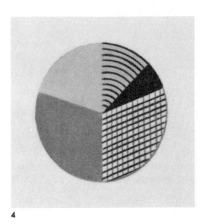

1

2

3

4

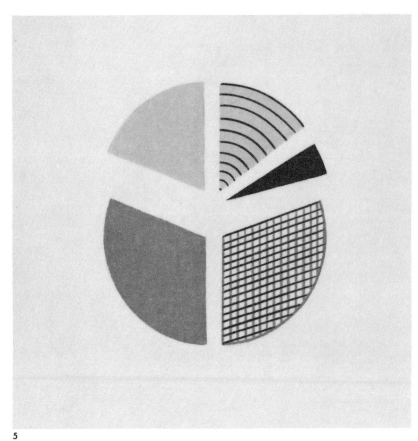

5

DIFFERENTIATED division shows each segment of the whole with an independent visual character, to separate the segments in relation to their individual meanings. Line, shade, value, and texture are used to accomplish this purpose within the context of the circular whole.

FIGURE 1. A simple division in which segments are differentiated by shade value, also creating an order of emphasis.

FIGURE 2. A differentiation of divided segments through the use of texture to prevent special emphasis through shade value.

FIGURE 3. Differentiated dividing lines to indicate different characteristics about the manner of the division itself.

FIGURE 4. Combined shade and textural description of segments to enhance differentiation and permit compound groupings.

FIGURE 5. A physical separation of the segments of figure 4 to further differentiate them in terms of their individual meanings. Here, the identity of the whole is minimized.

174

EMPHASIZED division shows one segment of the divided whole as an element of special importance by distinguishing it in terms of size, shade value, or physical separation. Similarly, the visual subordination of a segment can reduce its importance in the context of the whole.

FIGURE 1. The emphasis of one segment within an otherwise unified whole by extension beyond the edge of the whole. This extension is balanced by the darker shades of the remaining segments.

FIGURE 2. A similar emphasis by extension, reinforced by the absence of shade in remaining segments.

FIGURE 3. The emphasis of one segment by darker value and physical removal to convey a sense of detachment in its meaning.

FIGURE 4. The subordination of one segment by its absence from the whole.

FIGURE 5. The emphasis of one segment of a whole by its structure as an input element, and the subordination of another segment by a lighter shade value.

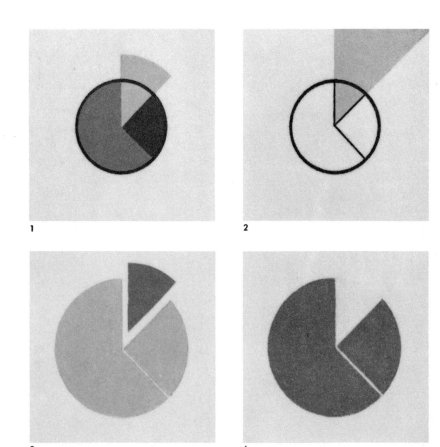

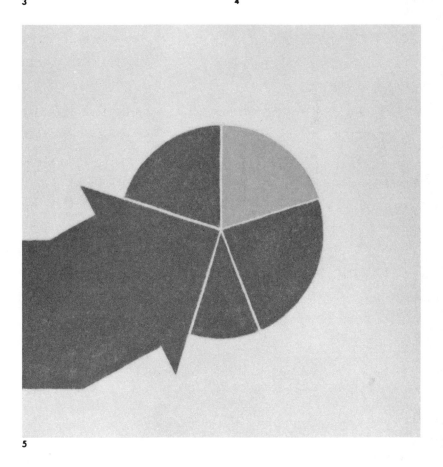

175

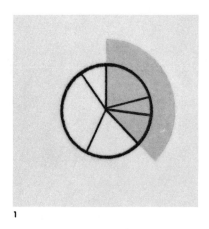

1

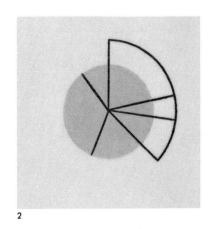

3

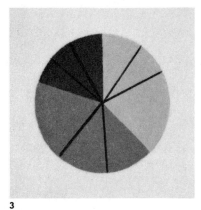

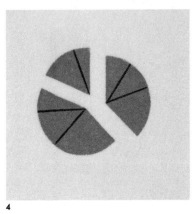

2

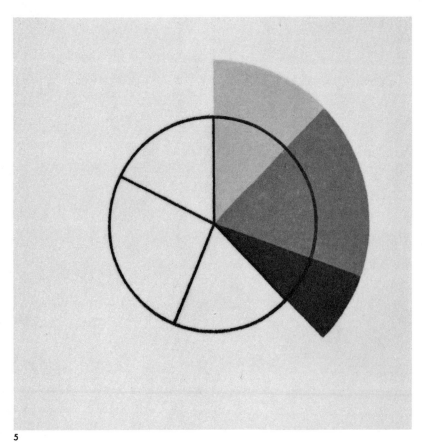

4

5

GROUPED division shows the organization of segments as sets of related elements or as individual elements that are subdivided. Here, form differentiation between major and minor divisions is important, in order to distinguish the different classes of segment meanings.

FIGURE 1. The emphasis of a segment grouping using an extended shade form.

FIGURE 2. The division structure of figure 1 emphasizing the whole as a solid shape while describing the segment grouping with subordinated outline.

FIGURE 3. The grouping of linear subdivisions within primary segments that are differentiated by varying shades of gray.

FIGURE 4. Segments physically separated into groupings of minor segments.

FIGURE 5. The outlined segments of a whole in which one of the segments is subdivided into minor segments by differentiated shades, which also act as an extended whole to define the parts as a grouping.

VARIABLE division shows segments whose dividing lines are either generalized or widened in form, to express a possible range in the proportional quantities of the segments. Such areas of variability can be shown either as form gaps or as areas of overlap which either one of the adjoining segments could occupy.

FIGURE 1. A simple division of components using shade form to show a definite range of variability for the dividing lines.

FIGURE 2. The same segments showing an indefinite range of variability by graduated shading.

FIGURE 3. The division of an emphasized whole into variable segments whose dividing lines are merely generalized. Here, the division is presented as merely tentative in nature.

FIGURE 4. An overlapping of division segments to indicate the possible extent of each segment.

FIGURE 5. An indefinite division of a whole into segments whose general areas can be identified but whose exact boundaries are unstated.

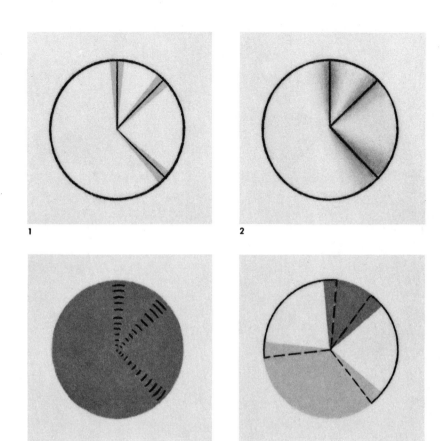

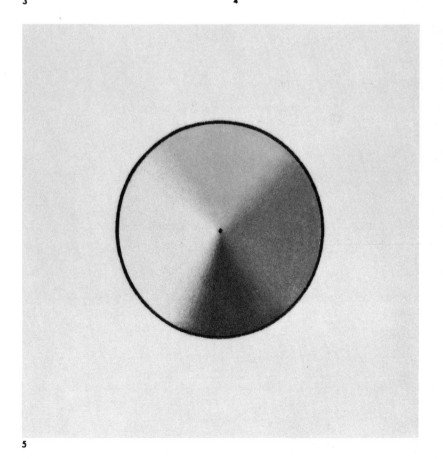

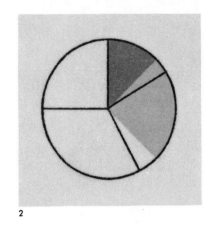

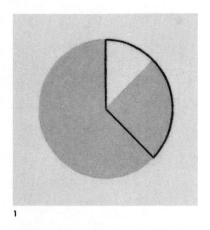

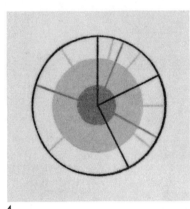

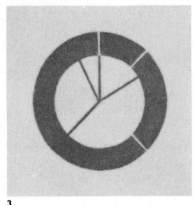

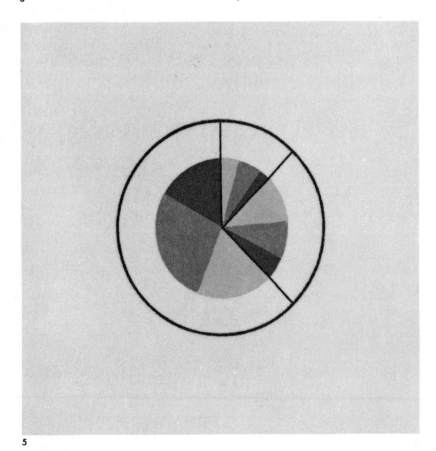

COMPOUND division shows the overlapping of segments to describe areas of joint meaning in relation to the subject elements they represent. Form differentiation is essential, since each of the overlapping segments must be clearly identifiable to convey the sense of a compound division.

FIGURE 1. A compound division showing line and shaded segments overlapping in an area of joint meaning.

FIGURE 2. An outlined division in which two shaded segments form a compound with two of the outline segments.

FIGURE 3. A compound division shown through the use of a double circumference which indicates overlapping segments.

FIGURE 4. A multiple circumference which permits three levels of overlapping segment meanings.

FIGURE 5. A compound circumference in which primary divisions overlap their secondary segments.

EXTENDED division quantifies the segments of a whole in terms of both the radius and the circumference measurements. While the circumference remains a proportional or percentage measurement, the radial measurement is in absolute numerical values. This permits dual quantification of subject elements in which one of the factors is a percentage value.

FIGURE 1. A simple extended division of segments emphasizing the unity of the whole.

FIGURE 2. A differentiation of the segments of figure 1 to characterize each of the individual elements and to emphasize one as black.

FIGURE 3. A compound extended division in which outlined segments are combined with the shade segments of figure 1.

FIGURE 4. Segments of figure 1 that are subdivided to show a pair of percentage components.

FIGURE 5. A complex extended division of segments, each of which is subdivided into three component quantities of the absolute amount factor.

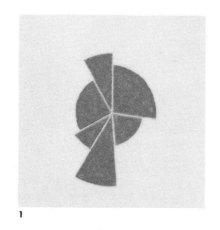
1

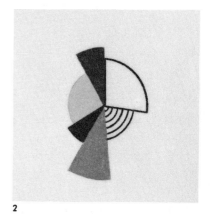
2

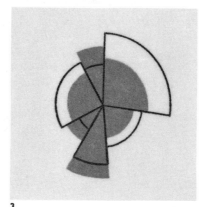
3

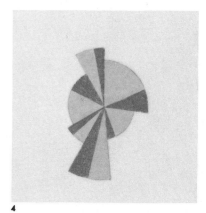
4

5

179

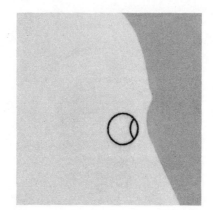

VII

TO SHOW *WHERE*

Where something is concerns its natural area, its environmental location, or its position with respect to other individual elements. To a great extent, these three aspects are related to one another. In fact, differences between them often seem to disappear in practice. An area can have a specific location; a location can be part of a network of positions; and a position can also occupy an area in the natural environment. What differentiates these aspects is the underlying view which guides each toward a specific communicative emphasis in showing *where* something is. In each case, the idea receives a different focus. For this reason, area, location, and position will be considered here as separate communicative aims and explored as primary problem areas.

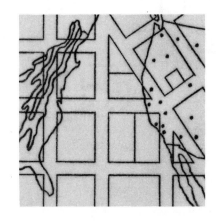

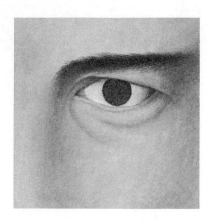

PHYSICAL

FORMALIZED

CHARACTERIZED

CIRCUMSTANTIAL

SEPARATED

Area concerns the space occupied by a subject in relation to its natural surroundings. In the graphic figure, the area and its surroundings can be shown in terms of their *physical* features, or they can be *formalized* to represent the essential structure of the subject. The form of an area can also be *characterized* to represent natural qualities that are not necessarily apparent. Areas affected by *circumstantial* conditions can be shown as well as areas which have been *separated* from their normal context for clarification. The following figure models represent design solutions to specific problems in these areas.

PHYSICAL area shows the natural features of a place in terms of its local surroundings. The area itself may have specifically defined boundaries, or it may occupy an indefinite space that has no exact visual edge. Since physical area is represented in terms of natural reality, an imaginary light source for graduated shading is necessary.

FIGURE 1. A physical description of mountain areas in the United States (see page 45).

FIGURE 2. A physical representation of an irregular seacoast emphasizing edge description.

FIGURE 3. A physical description of mountain and urban areas within a geographic region. Here, a variety of textural qualities as well as graduated shading are used to describe the subject elements.

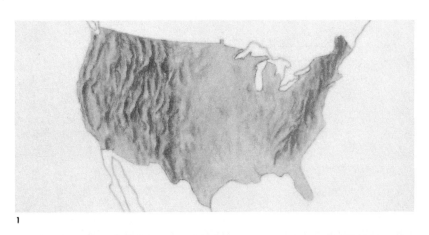

1

2

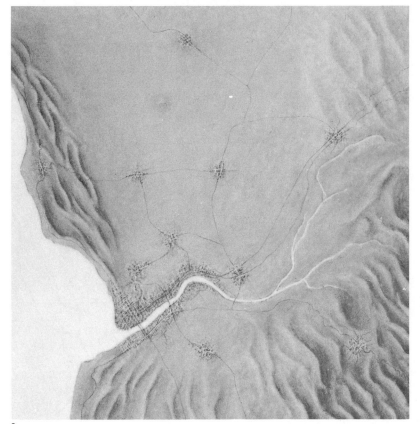

3

183

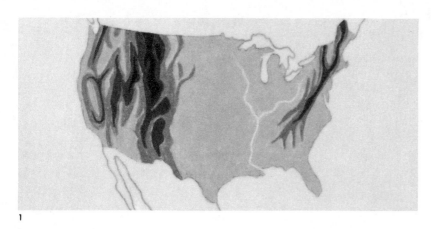

1

2

FORMALIZED area shows the structural nature of a place in terms of its essential characteristics, replacing natural features with simplified form that generalizes rather than reproduces the subject image. Here, technical clarity is more important than visual reality.

FIGURE 1. A formalized representation of mountain areas in the United States showing four levels of physical altitude with differentiated shade values.

FIGURE 2. A waterfront area formalized as a silhouette to emphasize only the dock area as an edge.

FIGURE 3. A diagrammatic representation of mountain areas in a region formalized as differentiated gray lines which identify land contours at several designated altitudes.

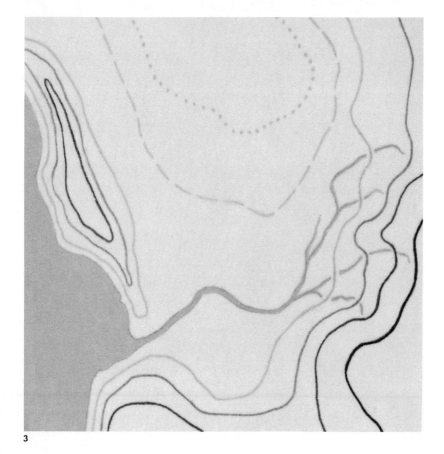

3

CHARACTERIZED areas can show natural qualities or properties of a locale which are not physically apparent in its geography or surface structure. Agricultural areas would be one example. Symbolic differentiation is necessary to such characterization. It generally utilizes shade values and textural patterns, since the shape of the area is automatically determined by the subject matter.

FIGURE 1. Specific economic areas of the United States characterized by shades and textures as assigned symbols whose meanings are defined by a key.

FIGURE 2. Areas of natural growth characterized by merging textures which indicate gradual subject change from one area to the next. An even color value is maintained for visual continuity.

FIGURE 3. A complex version of the concept of figure 1 showing economic (or other) areas in a region in terms of characterization. Here, overlapping areas are represented as well as differentiated areas that are otherwise related by common shade value or pattern.

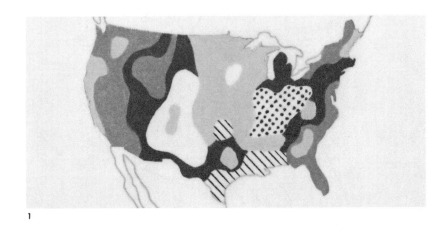

1

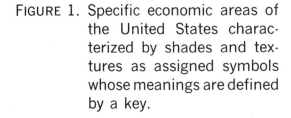

2

3

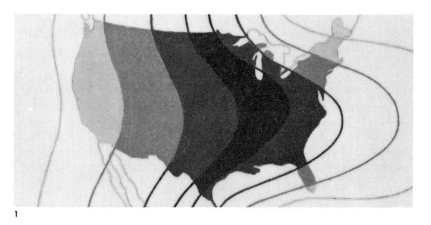

1

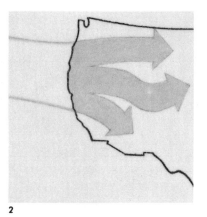

2

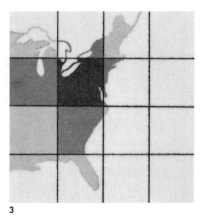

3

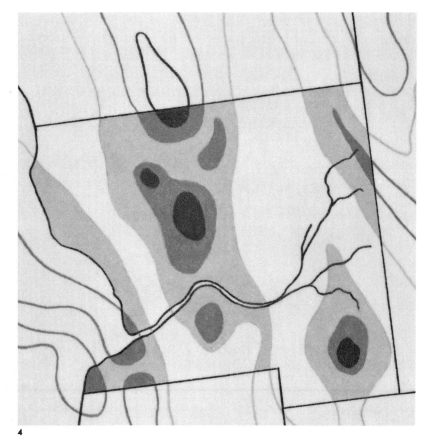

4

CIRCUMSTANTIAL areas are those which are defined by the nature of environmental conditions, or circumstances, and which affect the physical locale where they occur. Weather and temperature conditions are two examples. In representing such areas, it is necessary to maintain visual differentiation between the affecting circumstances and the natural environment to which they are directly related.

FIGURE 1. Differentiation of conditions affecting the United States by shades which cover only the land mass, while their defining contours extend beyond to indicate the scope of the conditions.

FIGURE 2. Conditions in motion in which directions of flow are indicated.

FIGURE 3. Natural circumstances organized in terms of a grid system, using shade values as in figure 1.

FIGURE 4. Environmental conditions affecting a region shown in solid shade description only within a bordered area of the region (as in figure 1).

SEPARATED areas are physically dissociated from one another to identify and represent their meanings in a more clarified form. Such separation can permit physical reorganization, removal of unnecessary areas, or enlargement of specific areas which require detailed description.

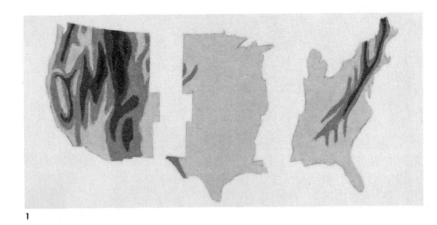

FIGURE 1. The separation and the reorganization of the land mass of the United States to clearly identify three major subject areas.

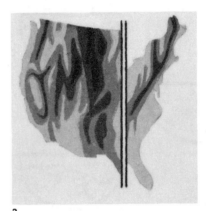

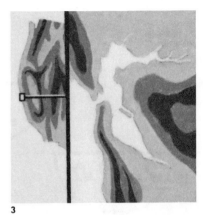

FIGURE 2. The removal of a central geographic area to show only the mountainous areas of the United States.

FIGURE 3. An enlargement of a small geographic area to show its structural details.

FIGURE 4. An enlargement of a small regional area to define its exact nature as a physical place. Here, texture is a primary vocabulary tool for the description of natural details.

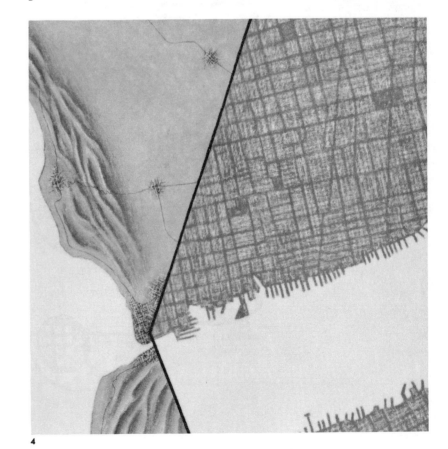

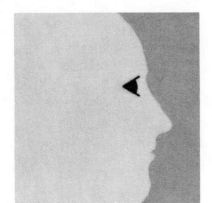

LOCATION

RELATED

DIFFERENTIATED

DESCRIBED

ROUTE

NETWORK

BOUNDARY

AREA

COMPOUND

MOVEMENT

QUANTIFIED

ENLARGED

Location concerns the spatial relationship between a subject and its overall environment. In the graphic figure, the environment acts as a frame of reference for the subject, which is usually minimized in size to focus its location. Subject elements can be *related* in character, or *differentiated* (as symbols), depending on their meaning. They can also be *described* in terms of their physical shapes. *Route* locations can be shown as well as *network* locations formed by routes and stations. The subject environment can be subdivided to show *boundary* locations, and subdivisions can be used as an environment to define *area* locations. Independent element patterns can be integrated as *compound* locations. *Movement* can also be expressed in relation to route locations. Locations can be *quantified*, or they can be *enlarged* to show location details. The following figure models represent design solutions to specific problems in these areas.

RELATED location shows focal subject elements of similar meaning in terms of the overall environment. While location elements such as points can be identical in their structure, their visual role can change in close association with each other where they begin to act as a unified mass. In such cases, the mass itself can be represented by an enlarged form of the same structure, such as a dot, in order to formalize the image for clarity.

FIGURE 1. City locations, as black points, within a subordinated gray outline of the United States (see page 46).

FIGURE 2. A pattern of subject locations whose density at certain places tends to describe shape configurations.

FIGURE 3. The generalization of dense locations as larger dots to compensate for the lack of space needed to clearly show the correct number of points.

FIGURE 4. Population distribution in a region represented by points and larger dots (to show concentrations) which are scaled in proportion to the number of people they represent.

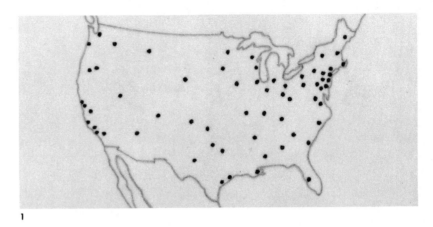

1

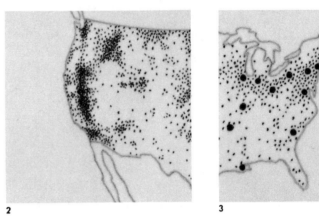

2   3

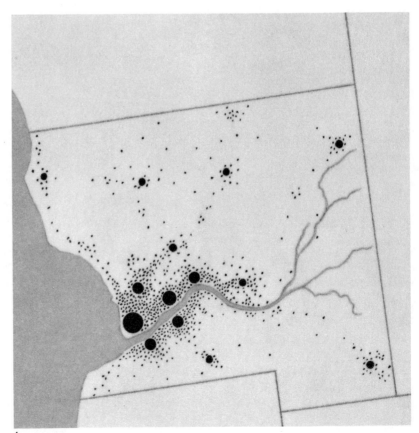

4

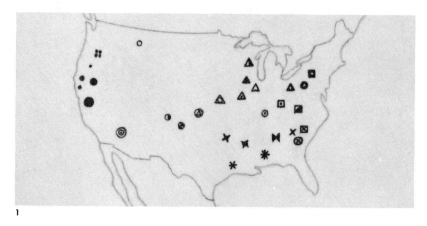

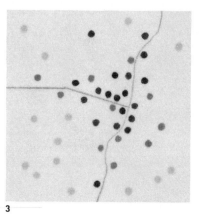

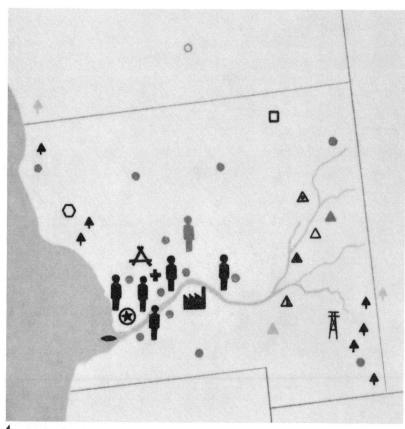

DIFFERENTIATED location shows elements of dissimilar meaning in spatial relation to their environment. Such locations can be shown with associative or conventional symbols, or by symbolic forms whose meanings are assigned by key. Since precise location is an aim, symbolic differentiation takes place on a small scale to maintain the focal quality of the elements.

FIGURE 1. The locations of various subject elements in the United States, differentiated by the form structure of assigned symbols.

FIGURE 2. The locations of certain subject elements in a locale, expressed through differentiated associative symbols.

FIGURE 3. Locations of different kinds of a common subject, through assigned dot symbols of varying shade values.

FIGURE 4. A complex pattern of locations using associative, conventional, and assigned symbols represented in both black and shaded form to differentiate a broad variety of subject element meanings.

DESCRIBED location shows subject elements which have a definite physical shape in relation to that of the surrounding environment. As location symbols, they retain this shape identity and thus often serve to describe an area as well as a location.

FIGURE 1. Specific locations of subject elements in the United States, described in terms of their geographic shapes.

FIGURE 2. Locations of elements of a subject which are joined as a common form; and which also constitute an area.

FIGURE 3. A pattern of described locations differentiated in character by varying shade values.

FIGURE 4. A complex pattern of described locations within a region, showing primary, secondary, and anticipated locations with black, shaded, and outline form.

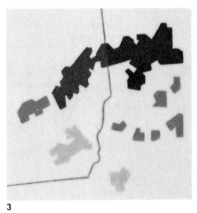

1

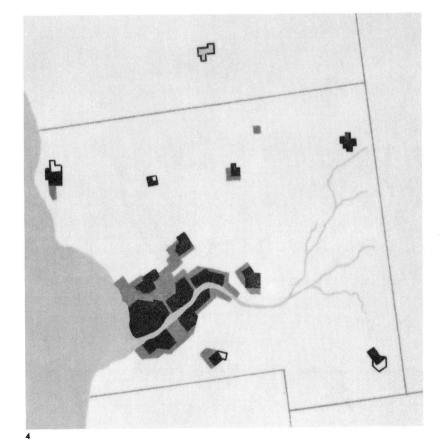

2

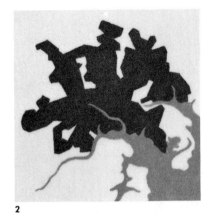

3

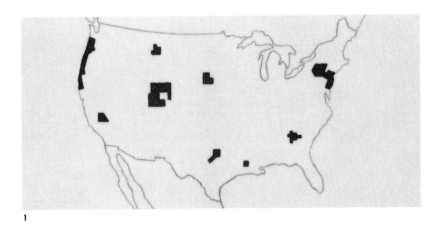

4

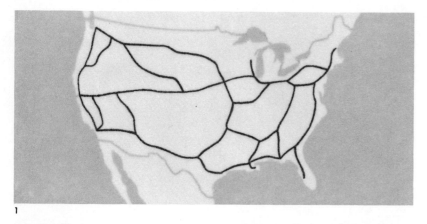

1

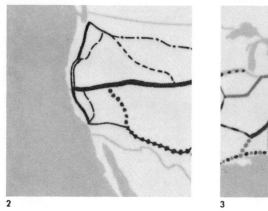

2

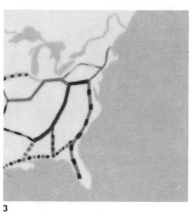

3

4

ROUTE location shows subject elements which act as linear extensions and show directional patterns in relation to the overall environment. While a route can be a purely descriptive formalization of a physical subject, such as a road, it can also act as a symbol to identify the nature of a route subject, such as a railroad. Here, the form vocabulary is mainly linear.

FIGURE 1. A simple pattern of road locations in the United States, represented by formalized description.

FIGURE 2. A pattern of dissimilar routes differentiated by linear structures which act as assigned symbols.

FIGURE 3. A pattern of dissimilar route types differentiated by structure and shade value.

FIGURE 4. A complex route pattern in a region showing highways, projected highways, classes of roads, and railroads, with a variety of assigned and conventional linear symbols.

NETWORK location shows an integrated pattern of routes and station elements in relation to their environment. The station elements can be formalized, symbolized, or described, depending on the need. As an image, network is essentially a problem in line and focal form (point and small shape).

FIGURE 1. A network of descriptive road routes and station symbols (cities) in the United States, contrasting black point and line elements against white and gray environmental shapes.

FIGURE 2. A simple network in which routes are symbolized as straight connecting links between descriptive station forms (cities).

FIGURE 3. Another symbolic network showing station elements as assigned symbols with three modes of meaning.

FIGURE 4. A complex example of a regional network showing three modes of stations and four kinds of routes within a descriptive context.

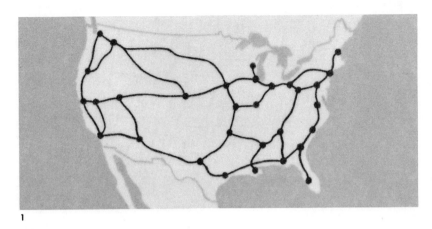

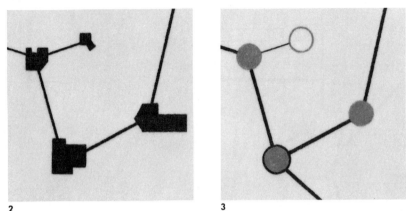

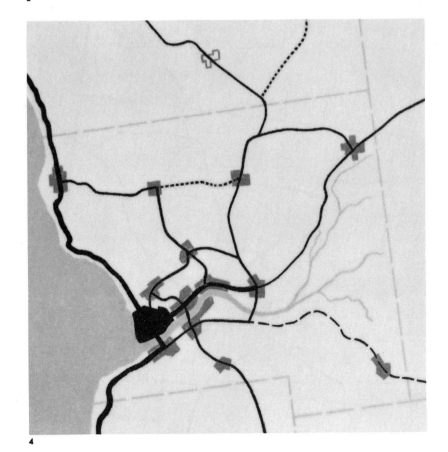

193

1

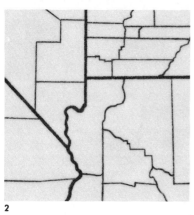

2

3

4

BOUNDARY location shows subject elements which, like routes, act as linear extensions in relation to the overall environment. They usually represent subjects such as the borders of political subdivisions. Here, forms which usually act as a subordinate frame of reference are shown as the primary subject in relation to a larger geographic and/or political environment.

FIGURE 1. State boundaries in the United States.

FIGURE 2. County boundaries shown in relation to intersecting state boundaries represented by wider black lines.

FIGURE 3. The same county boundaries in relation to state boundaries, differentiated by shade value to permit uniformly fine lines for accuracy.

FIGURE 4. A framework of major and minor boundaries shown as gray to act as a subordinate frame of reference for the black route network superimposed over it.

AREA location shows a subject place in specific relation to a detailed geographic and/or political frame of reference which intersects it and defines the exact locations of its various parts. If the subject area is general, its shape can be represented by borders which are a part of the environmental framework, to enhance its locational identity.

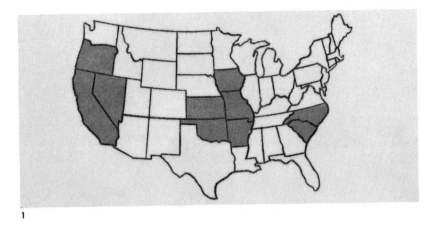

FIGURE 1. Three shaded area locations in the United States shown in relation to a state boundary framework.

FIGURE 2. Five areas of three subject types shown by varying shade values within a New England county framework.

FIGURE 3. Six areas, differentiated as subjects by textural patterns, shown in the county environment of figure 2.

FIGURE 4. Six areas within a region visually characterized by shade and texture in terms of subject differences and similarities. The areas are located within a framework of district boundaries.

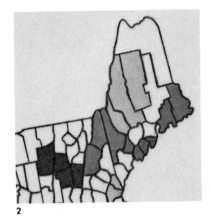

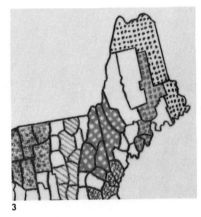

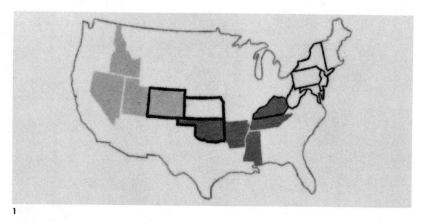

1

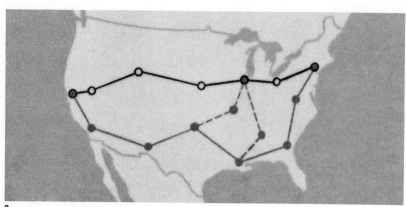

2

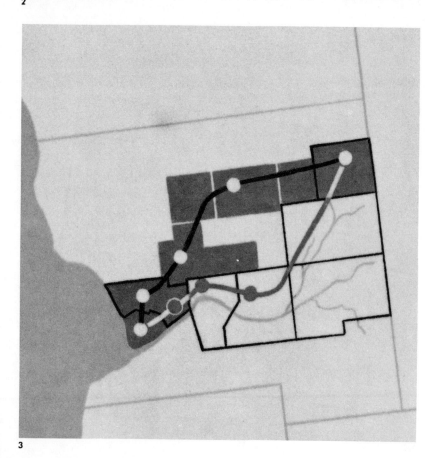

3

COMPOUND location shows two or more subjects of independent meaning in joint combination with each other, in relation to an environment. Compound subject elements are usually expressed in overlapping arrangements which require a sharply differentiated form vocabulary in order for each member of the compound to maintain an independent visual identity.

FIGURE 1. A multiple compound of four subject identities representing joint area locations in the United States.

FIGURE 2. A compound route network within the United States showing three of the stations occupied jointly by primary (black) and secondary (gray) routes.

FIGURE 3. A compound network which includes a compound representation of district areas through which the network passes. The two network routes and their related areas are differentiated by a wide vocabulary of complimentary forms.

MOVEMENT location indicates the motion of a subject over a network route in relation to its environment. Both the direction and the path of the movement can be shown, as well as its quality or quantity. Visual differentiation between the active movement form (usually an arrow symbol) and the inactive network structure over which it passes is necessary (see also pages 122 and 123).

FIGURE 1. Directions of movement over a located route network in the United States.

FIGURE 2. Movement patterns differentiated in quality with respect to the character of the routes over which they pass.

FIGURE 3. A route network in which the movement pattern is indicated simply by arrowhead symbols.

FIGURE 4. A movement pattern within a regional network showing relative volume of traffic by width of shaded lines. Here, direction is not indicated since traffic is understood to be moving in both directions.

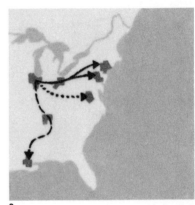

1

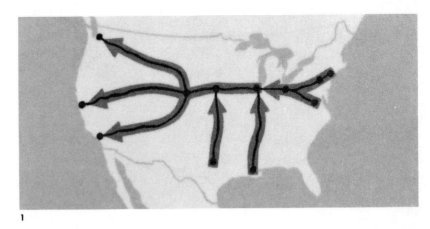

2

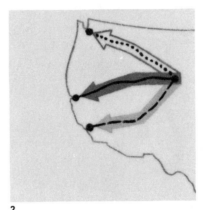

3

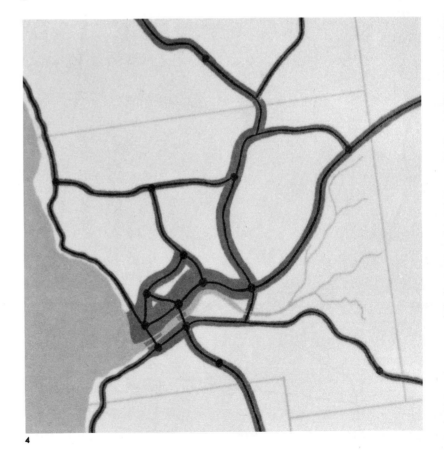

4

197

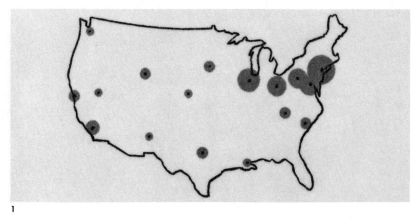

1

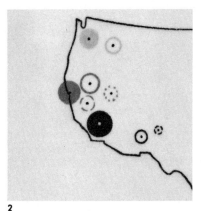

2

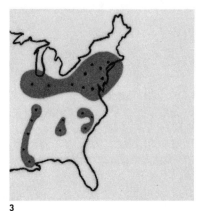

3

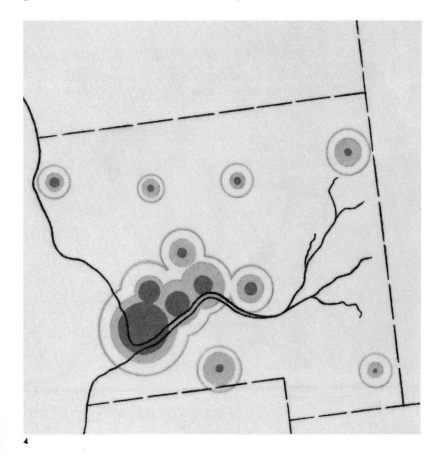

4

QUANTIFIED location shows the quantitative magnitude of subject elements in relation to an environment. While the subjects can be related or differentiated in identity, their terms of visual measurement must be constant in order to show a meaningful quantitative comparison.

FIGURE 1. Quantified locations in the United States showing the relative magnitude associated with each location as a circular gray area.

FIGURE 2. A pattern of located quantities differentiated in identity but related in terms of their circular magnitude.

FIGURE 3. Four patterns of locations whose magnitudes are expressed in combination with one another as generalized quantitative form.

FIGURE 4. Three orders of magnitude shown in relation to each location in a regional pattern. The exact locations are implied (as centers) by the concentric rings.

ENLARGED location shows the scaled expansion of the form of the subject, which is otherwise related to a specific environment. Enlargement permits the visual representation of detailed features which can otherwise not be shown within the scale of the environmental context.

FIGURE 1. An enlargement of the Chicago section of a railroad network which otherwise encompasses the entire United States.

FIGURE 2. An enlargement of a located city showing a position within its street pattern.

FIGURE 3. Scale enlargement can also be enabled by the removal of unnecessary areas, in this case, to clarify network terminal patterns.

FIGURE 4. Enlargement of a city location to show a detail of the terminating phase of a route movement.

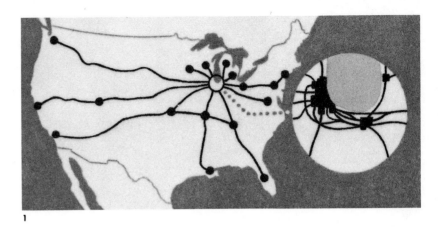

1

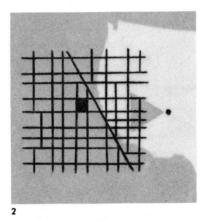

2

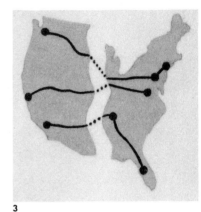

3

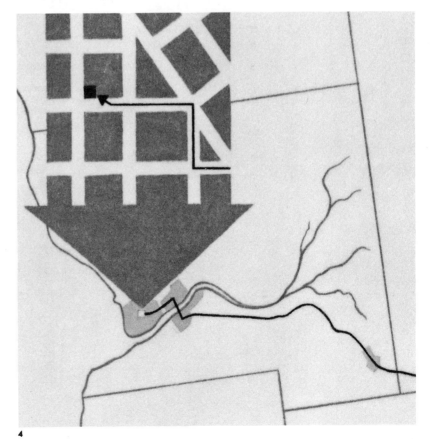

4

POSITION

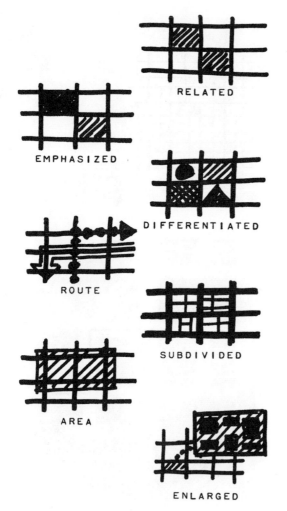

EMPHASIZED

RELATED

DIFFERENTIATED

ROUTE

SUBDIVIDED

AREA

ENLARGED

Position concerns the spatial relation of a subject element to other elements within an area. In the graphic figure, position is generally shown within a pattern of associated elements, for example, a pattern of streets and blocks. The identified positions within this pattern can be *related* in character or *emphasized* with respect to their importance. They can also be *differentiated* in terms of their various meanings. Position can be expressed as *route,* or it can be *subdivided* in terms of secondary positions. Position elements can also be shown in relation to a defined *area,* or *enlarged* to permit description of details. The following figure models represent design solutions to specific problems in these areas.

RELATED position elements are those whose meanings are parallel and are, therefore, visually represented with a similar form character. Generally, the surrounding elements of the pattern which are not identified as specific positions are shown in visually subordinated form.

FIGURE 1. Four positions of similar character (black) shown in relation to a pattern of negative (white) elements created by the gray street structure (see page 47).

FIGURE 2. A reversal of the gray pattern of figure 1, to associate the black positions with the street blocks.

FIGURE 3. The pattern of figure 1 showing black elements in terms of their natural details.

FIGURE 4. Four element positions related by similar shade value and by a linear street structure.

FIGURE 5. The positions of similar (black) subjects grouped within a complex street pattern.

201

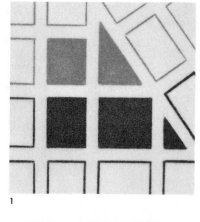
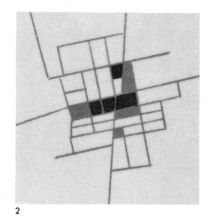

1

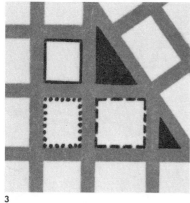
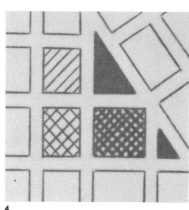

2

3

4

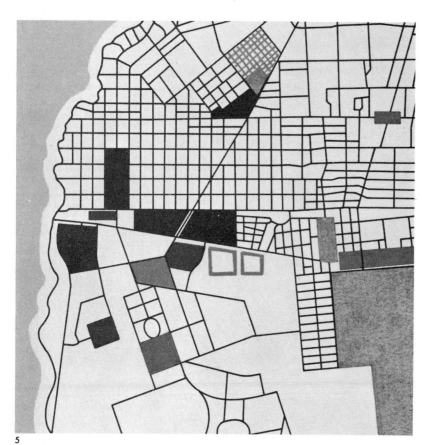

5

EMPHASIZED position shows subject elements within an order of relative importance, using shade and physical structure to convey a specific degree of visual impact in each subject. Elements of lesser importance can be visually subordinated in relation to others, by the removal of emphatic form qualities.

FIGURE 1. Emphasis (black) and subordination (gray) of positions within a pattern of street blocks which are further subordinated as outline.

FIGURE 2. An order of importance as in figure 1, within a formalized linear street pattern.

FIGURE 3. An order of importance through position structure, ranging from solid black to dotted black outline.

FIGURE 4. An order of textural importance ranging from solid and close to open.

FIGURE 5. A pattern of relative emphasis through the combined use of shade value, structure, and texture within a complex, formalized street pattern.

DIFFERENTIATED position shows subject elements of different orders of meaning, characterizing them with a full form vocabulary. As differentiated positions, they can act descriptively (as block shapes) and at the same time symbolically, with associative, conventional, or assigned meanings.

FIGURE 1. A variety of differentiated block positions shown as assigned symbols within a larger pattern of block elements.

FIGURE 2. Symbolized block positions shown within a formalized street pattern.

FIGURE 3. Associative and conventional symbols used within the street pattern of figure 1.

FIGURE 4. A modified version of figure 1 in which unidentified block elements act in close association with position blocks.

FIGURE 5. A wide assortment of symbolized positions within a complex, formalized street pattern.

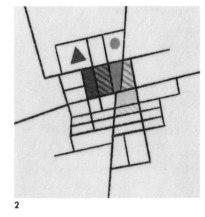

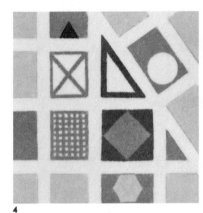

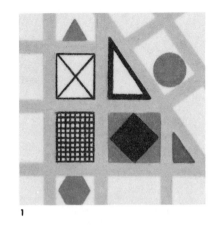

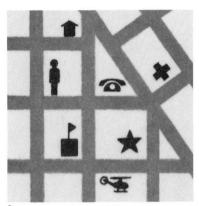

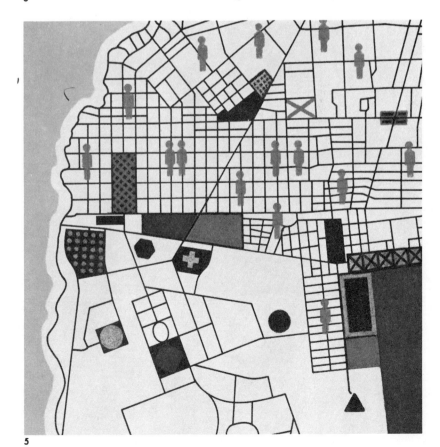

203

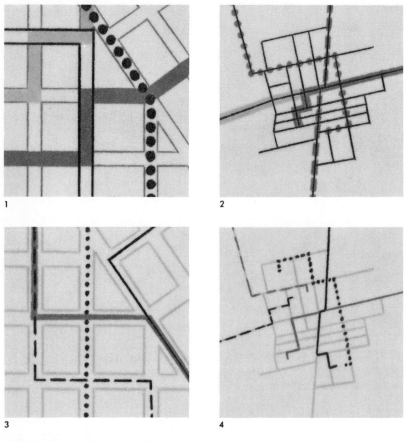

1

2

3

4

ROUTE position shows subject elements which act in a linear pattern, usually in relation to other linear structures or spaces such as streets. In such cases, the street forms are characterized in the same way that the block forms between them are characterized to show non-linear positions.

FIGURE 1. A variety of route positions occupying a street pattern characterized with differentiated structures and shade values.

FIGURE 2. A formalized street pattern showing shaded route positions with differentiated linear structures.

FIGURE 3. Routes within the street pattern of figure 1, acting as independent paths inside the street forms, rather than as dependent characteristics of the streets themselves.

FIGURE 4. A shaded version of the street pattern of figure 2, using superimposed black structure and dark shade to define integral route positions.

FIGURE 5. A network of differentiated route positions which characterize elements of a complex street network.

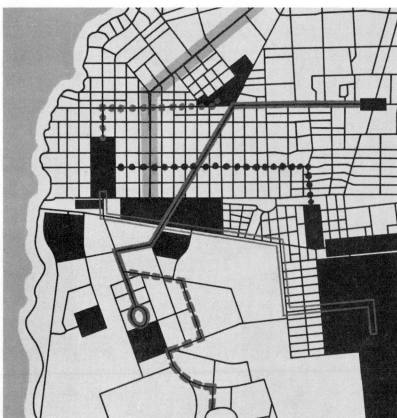

5

SUBDIVIDED position shows subject elements in terms of their secondary organization or internal structure. Within a given subject, such as a street network, each of the mutually complimentary patterns (in this case, the block pattern *vs.* the street pattern) may be shown as subdivided positions.

FIGURE 1. A subdivision of block elements identified as subject positions.

FIGURE 2. A subdivision of a formalized street pattern using black for primary and gray for secondary positions.

FIGURE 3. A subdivision of the street pattern of figure 1, showing primary (dark) and secondary (light) elements within a pattern of unidentified (white) block elements.

FIGURE 4. An identification of secondary street positions by emphasizing the primary streets with reinforcing shades.

FIGURE 5. Subdivision of a complex street pattern showing three levels of identity (wide black, narrow black, and gray).

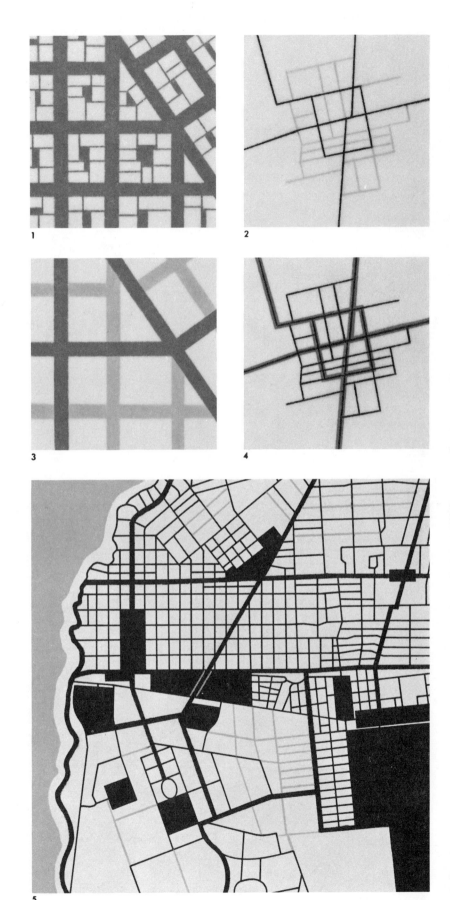

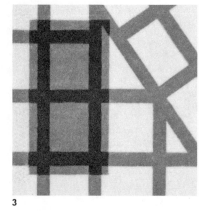

1

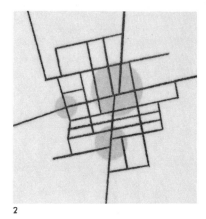

2

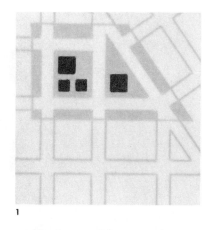

3

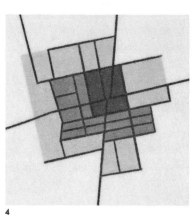

4

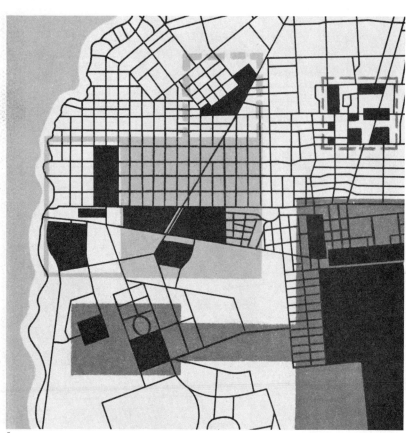

5

AREA position shows subject elements which are identified as a group by an enclosing form, usually a shape. The enclosing shape can differentiate as well as identify position groups, through shade and outline form. To disengage its own edges from those of surrounded forms, the enclosing shape often overlaps them.

FIGURE 1. An area position which includes two blocks and the black elements within them.

FIGURE 2. Three circular positions whose shaded forms identify intersection areas.

FIGURE 3. An area position which emphasizes two blocks and their adjacent streets.

FIGURE 4. Three area positions differentiated within an order of emphasis by shade values.

FIGURE 5. A complex pattern of area positions in which five differentiated enclosing forms also create and order of emphasis.

ENLARGED position shows subject elements or areas in an expanded scale to clarify or describe in detail features that would not otherwise, due to scale limitations, be evident. At the same time, the environmental pattern is necessary to show the spatial relation of the subject position to other elements.

FIGURE 1. An enlargement of a formalized street position to enable clear description of the blocks.

FIGURE 2. An enlargement of a block position to show the pattern of buildings it contains.

FIGURE 3. An enlargement of an eight block area position to show the pattern of buildings contained in each block.

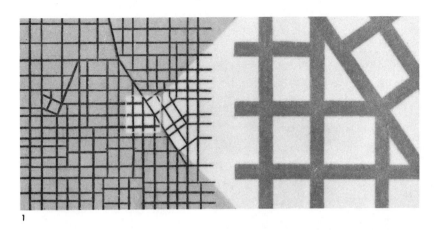

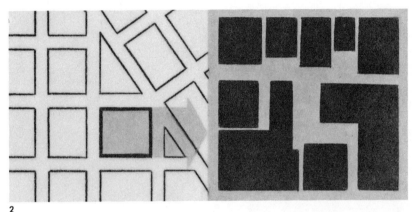

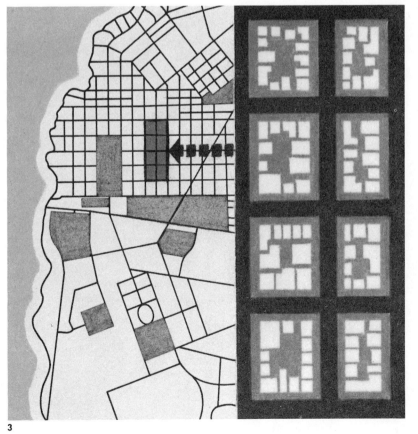

INDEX

RECEIVED FEB 0 8 1994